D1321264

TREVOR McDONALD
FAVOURITE POEMS

Trevor McDonald, popular newscaster and also Chairman of the Campaign for Better Use of the English Language, has now compiled an anthology of his favourite poetry from across the ages. The collection is based on material published in his regular Anthology column in the DAILY TELEGRAPH. It is a comprehensive introduction to the poetry of the English language, from Milton to Ted Hughes, from Britain and abroad. He has included both perennial favourites and less familiar but accessible poetry. Each poet is introduced with a concise history of their work and there is something to suit all tastes and moods.

TREVOR McDONALD

◆

FAVOURITE POEMS
The Daily Telegraph

Complete and Unabridged

CHARNWOOD
Leicester

First published in Great Britain in 1997 by
Michael O'Mara Books Limited
London

First Charnwood Edition
published 1999
by arrangement with
Michael O'Mara Books Limited
London

British Library CIP Data

McDonald, Trevor
    Favourite poems.—Large print ed.—
Charnwood library series
    1. English poetry 2. American poetry
    3. Large type books
    I. McDonald, Trevor II. Favourite poems
821'.008

ISBN 0–7089–9052–5

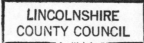

Published by
F. A. Thorpe (Publishing) Ltd.
Anstey, Leicestershire

Set by Words & Graphics Ltd.
Anstey, Leicestershire
Printed and bound in Great Britain by
T. J. International Ltd., Padstow, Cornwall

This book is printed on acid-free paper

For Jack

Acknowledgements

I would like to express my gratitude to Sarah Sands, Deputy Editor of the *Daily Telegraph*, and to her colleagues on the paper for all the assistance they have given me over many months in the selection and presentation of the poems in the *Telegraph*. Their unfailing courtesy and kindness made working for them a genuine pleasure. When the decision was made to publish an anthology, Vicky Unwin, Director of Enterprises at the *Telegraph*, took an interest in the project from start to finish and was always on hand to deal with my anxious questions with clarity and skill. In Sarah and Vicky I have found great friends. I owe a greater debt of gratitude than I can pay to my ITN colleague Pauline Heard. I am always terribly conscious of the fact that without her assistance so few of the many projects I undertake would be even remotely possible. Finally it was a pleasure to deal with publisher Michael O'Mara and the editor of this anthology, Stephanie Cooke. Nothing ever seemed too much of a problem for them. Together they made the preparation of this anthology a joy.

Table of Contents

Seamus Heaney

Preface

This anthology owes its existence to an invitation from the Editor of the *Daily Telegraph*, Charles Moore, that I contribute a weekly poem to his paper.

Few assignments have excited me more or given me greater pleasure for such a sustained period.

For as long as I can remember, poetry has been part of my life. I have always regarded that as a matter of good fortune. Memories of my earliest childhood days are much too dim and distant now to be anything but unreliable, but I grew up with the notion, reinforced by family lore, that my mother began reciting her favourite poems to me while I was still 'mewling and puking' in her arms. Of these I would have remembered almost nothing at all, had my mother not followed up her earlier recitations by reminding me throughout her long life how competent she was at remembering the works of her favourite poets. Impressively therefore she would recite entire stanzas from Milton, Byron, Tennyson and Kipling. It has never ceased to give me frissons of delight that in doing research for my *Daily Telegraph* column I still encounter lines spoken to me by my mother, and lines which I consequently came to know by heart, although, naggingly, neither of us could be sure of their provenance. One of them I encountered by chance only a few weeks ago: Longfellow's *A psalm of life*, in which the poet exhorts his readers as my mother relentlessly exhorted me, to make something of my time at school and of my life:

> Lives of great men all remind us
> We can make our lives sublime,
> And, departing, leave behind us
> Footprints on the sands of time;

For my mother that became something of a creed, especially as the poem began with the somewhat pious, quasi-religious sentiments about life being real and earnest, and 'Dust thou art and dust returnest.' The seeds of interest in poetry sowed at home were assiduously cultivated by my schools. Many of the themes and places alluded to in the poems we were taught were quite alien to us, but we were made to study them and learn them by heart anyway. One of the abiding memories of my early school life is of standing in an assembly area in a class of about twenty or thirty, and with the temperature in the eighties, reciting, in what passed for unison, Wordsworth's *Daffodils*. I've frequently reflected since that passers-by, hearing us without actually seeing our class, must have been at best amused or at worst terribly perplexed.

The result of all this is that I acquired and luckily never lost an interest in poetry. Making the selection for this anthology, therefore, has been a labour of love. Anthologists are usually required to justify the selections they make. That is as it should be. I can do little more than say that the poems I have chosen are, for a variety of reasons, favourites. Some choices are made because of my affection for the poets; others because I have particularly liked a poem, regardless of how little I know of its author. From the number of letters and less formal comments I get from *Daily Telegraph* readers, I know they are the favourites of large sections of the population too. That gives me great pleasure. But I am acutely aware that anthologists have a wider duty to introduce their readers to less familiar but accessible poetry, and to make their selection fairly representative of that great body of English poetry which we are so fortunate to have inherited. I hope that in at least some way I have managed to do that. But of course I know too that among the selections I've made are many poems that have touched my soul, those which, as Wordsworth says about the landscape that inspired *Tintern Abbey*, are poems that:

> . . . in lonely rooms and 'mid the din
> Of towns and cities, I have owed to them
> In hours of weariness, sensations sweet,
> Felt in the blood, and felt along the heart
> And passing even into my purer mind,
> With tranquil restoration.

That in essence is what poetry means to me. At its best, good poetry transports its readers to worlds never dreamt of. It distils, refines and lifts the language to the heights of otherwise inexpressible beauty. Thus, for example, do the words of Auden's *Lullaby* light up the senses and fall gently upon the heart with such delight:

Time and fevers burn away
Individual beauty from
Thoughtful children, and the grave
Proves the child ephemeral:

The sweeping grandeur of Wordsworth and brilliant precision of Eliot were as much a part of my childhood as the inspirational verse of Tennyson's *Ulysses,* urging restlessly that life must be drunk to the lees because:

Tho' much is taken, much abides; and tho'
We are not now that strength which in old days
Moved earth and heaven; that which we are, we are;
One equal temper of heroic hearts,
Made weak by time and fate, but strong in will
To strive, to seek, to find, and not to yield.

I can go on and on. But suffice it to say that these are a few glimpses of the thoughts and the poems I hope to share. I read recently that one anthologist felt it was totally unnecessary to entice his readers by sharing with them any of the background and the history against which the poems were written. This of course is a matter of personal preference, but I have done it because my appreciation of a multitude of poems has been enhanced by some knowledge of the poets and of the temper of the time in which they wrote. Thus did William Butler Yeats write, at a fateful juncture in the history of Irish nationalism, in *Easter 1916* of:

MacDonagh and MacBride
And Connolly and Pearse
Now and in time to be,
Wherever green is worn,
Are changed, changed utterly:
A terrible beauty is born.

Presenting my favourite poems in this collection has been a challenge and a joy. The challenge has been mine alone. I hope the joy is shared by many.

Trevor McDonald 1997

Sir Walter Ralegh (1554 – 1618)

Ralegh is better known as a soldier and explorer than a poet. His amazing life has been the subject of many an adventure film and the hoary tale of his throwing a splendid cloak over a puddle for Queen Elizabeth I is known to every schoolboy. However, the death of Elizabeth also sealed Ralegh's fate when James I had him executed on false charges of treason.

Walsingham

'As you came from the holy land
    of Walsingham,
Met you not with my true love
    By the way as you came?'

'How shall I know your true love,
    That have met many one
As I went to the holy land,
    That have come, that have gone?'

'She is neither white nor brown,
    But as the heavens fair,
There is none hath a form so divine
    In the earth or the air.'

'Such an one did I meet, good Sir,
    Such an angelic face,
Who like a queen, like a nymph did appear
    By her gait, by her grace.'

1

'She hath left me here all alone,
    All alone as unknown,
Who sometimes did me lead with herself,
    And me loved as her own.'

'What's the cause that she leaves you alone
    And a new way doth take,
Who loved you once as her own
    And her joy did you make?'

'I have loved her all my youth,
    But now old as you see,
Love likes not the falling fruit
    From the withered tree.

'Know that Love is a careless child,
    And forgets promise past;
He is blind, he is deaf when he list
    And in faith never fast.

'His desire is a dureless content
    And a trustless joy;
He is won with a world of despair
    And is lost with a toy.

'Of womenkind such indeed is the love
    Or the word love abused,
Under which many childish desires
    And conceits are excused.

'But true Love is a durable fire
    In the mind ever burning;
Never sick, never old, never dead,
    From itself never turning.'

All the world's a stage
(On the life of man)
What is our life? A play of passion,
Our mirth the music of division.
Our mothers' wombs the tiring-houses be,
Where we are dressed for this short comedy.
Heaven the judicious sharp spectator is,
That sits and marks still who doth act amiss.
Our graves that hide us from the searching sun
Are like drawn curtains when the play is done.
Thus march we, playing, to our latest rest.
Only we die in earnest, that's no jest.

William Shakespeare (1564 – 1616)
Shakespeare's sonnets are gems of the English language. Yet since their publication in the early seventeenth century, they have been steeped in controversy. What is not in doubt is the range of human emotion that they express — from love, despair and the pain of loss and longing, to the conflict between platonic love and sexual desire. The big questions are: were they inspired by emotional crisis in the poet's life and, if so, who were the objects of such passionate devotion? We may never know, but the poems remain compelling works of beauty. Shakespeare wrote more than 150 sonnets, but incorporated others in longer poems.

Sweet music's power
Orpheus with his lute made trees
And the mountain tops that freeze
   Bow themselves when he did sing:

To his music plants and flowers
Ever sprung; as sun and showers
    There had made a lasting spring.

Every thing that heard him play,
Even the billows of the sea,
    Hung their heads and then lay by.
In sweet music is such art,
Killing care and grief of heart
    Fall asleep, or hearing, die.

Sonnet 116
Let me not to the marriage of true minds
Admit impediments. Love is not love
Which alters when it alteration finds,
Or bends with the remover to remove:
O, no! it is an ever-fixèd mark
That looks on tempests and is never shaken;
It is the star to every wandering bark,
Whose worth's unknown, although his height be taken.
Love's not Time's fool, though rosy lips and cheeks,
Within his bending sickle's compass come;
Love alters not with his brief hours and weeks,
But bears it out even to the edge of doom.
If this be error and upon me proved,
I never writ, nor no man ever loved.

From **The passionate pilgrim**
I
When my love swears that she is made of truth,
I do believe her, though I know she lies,

4

That she might think me some untutored youth,
Unskilful in the world's false forgeries.
Thus vainly thinking that she thinks me young,
Although I know my years be past the best,
I smiling credit her false-speaking tongue,
Outfacing faults in love with love's ill rest.
But wherefore says my love that she is young?
And wherefore say not I that I am old?
O, love's best habit is a soothing tongue,
And age, in love, loves not to have years told.
    Therefore I'll lie with love, and love with me,
    Since that our faults in love thus smothered be.

II
Two loves I have, of comfort and despair,
That like two spirits do suggest me still;
My better angel is a man right fair,
My worser spirit a woman coloured ill.
To win me soon to hell, my female evil
Tempteth my better angel from my side,
And would corrupt my saint to be a devil,
Wooing his purity with her fair pride.
And whether that my angel be turned fiend,
Suspect I may, yet not directly tell:
For being both to me, both to each friend,
I guess one angel in another's hell:
    The truth I shall not know, but live in
    doubt,
    Till my bad angel fire my good one out.

John Donne (1572 – 1631)
John Donne's place in history would have
been secure even had he never become a great
poet. He trained as a lawyer, became

Secretary to the Lord Keeper of the Great
Seal in 1598, and 22 years later, on becoming
Dean of St Paul's, achieved considerable fame
as a fiery preacher. His career as a poet began
before he went to the church, but there was
always a religious fervour to his poetry.

His early love poems shine with this
intensity, but they are also written with great
tenderness. He was the first and the most
important of the Metaphysical poets, his
influence was profound and although he never
achieved fame in his own lifetime, his
popularity has never lapsed.

The ecstasy
Where, like a pillow on a bed,
  A pregnant bank swelled up, to rest
The violet's reclining head,
  Sat we two, one another's best.

Our hands were firmly cemented
  With a fast balm, which thence did spring;
Our eye-beams twisted, and did thread
  Our eyes upon one double string;

So to entergraft our hands, as yet
  Was all our means to make us one,
And pictures in our eyes to get
  Was all our propagation.

As 'twixt two equal armies fate
  Suspends uncertain victory,
Our souls (which to advance their state
  Were gone out) hung 'twixt her and me.

And whilst our souls negotiate there,
  We like sepulchral statues lay;
All day the same our postures were,
  And we said nothing all the day.

If any, so by love refined
  That he soul's language understood,
And by good love were grown all mind,
  Within convenient distance stood,

He (though he knew not which soul spake,
  Because both meant, both spake the same)
Might thence a new concoction take,
  And part far purer than he came.

This ecstasy doth unperplex
  (We said) and tell us what we love,
We see by this, it was not sex,
  We see, we saw not what did move:

But as all several souls contain
  Mixture of things, they know not what,
Love these mixed souls doth mix again,
  And makes both one, each this and that.

A single violet transplant,
  The strength, the colour, and the size,
(All which before was poor and scant)
  Redoubles still, and multiplies.

When love with one another so
  Interinanimates two souls,
That abler soul, which thence doth flow,
  Defects of loneliness controls.

7

We then, who are this new soul, know
    Of what we are composed, and made,
For the atomies of which we grow
    Are souls, whom no change can invade.

But, O alas! so long, so far
    Our bodies why do we forbear?
They are ours, though they are not we; we are
    The intelligences, they the sphere.

We owe them thanks, because they thus,
    Did us, to us, at first convey,
Yielded their forces, sense, to us,
    Nor are dross to us, but allay.

On man heaven's influence works not so,
    But that it first imprints the air;
So soul into the soul may flow,
    Though it to body first repair.

As our blood labours to beget
    Spirits, as like souls as it can;
Because such fingers need to knit
    That subtle knot, which makes us man;

So must pure lovers' souls descend
    To affections, and to faculties,
Which sense may reach and apprehend,
    Else a great prince in prison lies.

To our bodies turn we then, that so
    Weak men on love revealed may look;
Love's mysteries in souls do grow,
    But yet the body is his book.

And if some lover, such as we,
  Have heard this dialogue of one,
Let him still mark us, he shall see
  Small change, when we're to bodies gone.

Lovers' infiniteness

If yet I have not all thy love,
Dear, I shall never have it all,
I cannot breathe one other sigh, to move,
Nor can entreat one other tear to fall;
And all my treasure, which should purchase
    thee,
Sighs, tears, and oaths, and letters, I have
    spent.
Yet no more can be due to me,
Than at the bargain made was meant:
If then thy gift of love were partial,
That some to me, some should to others fall,
Dear I shall never have thee all.

Or if then thou gavest me all,
All was but all, which thou hadst then;
But if, in thy heart, since, there be or shall
New love created be by other men,
Which have their stocks entire, and can in tears,
In sighs, in oaths, and letters outbid me,
This new love may beget new fears,
For this love was not vowed by thee.
And yet it was, thy gift being general;
The ground, thy heart, is mine; what ever shall
Grow there, dear, I should have it all.

Yet I would not have all yet;
He that hath all can have no more;

And since my love doth every day admit
New growth, thou shouldst have new rewards
    in store;
Thou canst not every day give me thy heart,
If thou canst give it, then thou never gavest it;
Love's riddles are that though thy heart depart,
It stays at home, and thou with losing savest it:
But we will have a way more liberal
Than changing hearts, to join them; so we
    shall
Be one, and one another's all.

Song
Sweetest love, I do not go
    For weariness of thee,
Nor in hope the world can show
    A fitter love for me:
    But since that I
Must die at last, 'tis best,
To use myself in jest
    Thus by feigned deaths to die.

Yesternight the sun went hence,
    And yet is here today
He hath no desire nor sense,
    Nor half so short a way;
        Then fear not me,
But believe that I shall make
Speedier journeys, since I take
    More wings and spurs than he.

Oh, how feeble is man's power,
    That if good fortune fall,
Cannot add another hour,

Nor a lost hour recall!
    But come bad chance,
And we join to it our strength,
And we teach it art and length,
    Itself o'er us to advance.

When thou sighest, thou sighest not wind,
    But sighest my soul away;
When thou weepest, unkindly kind,
    My life's blood doth decay.
        It cannot be
That thou lovest me, as thou sayest,
If in thine my life thou waste,
    Thou art the best of me.

Let not thy divining heart
    Forethink me any ill,
Destiny may take thy part
    And may thy fears fulfil.
        But think that we
Are but turned aside to sleep;
They who one another keep
    Alive, ne'er parted be.

The good-morrow
I wonder by my troth, what thou and I
    Did, till we loved? were we not weaned
        till then?
But sucked on country pleasures, childishly?
    Or snorted we in the seven sleepers' den?
'Twas so; But this, all pleasures fancies be.
    If ever any beauty I did see,
Which I desired, and got, 'twas but a dream
    of thee.

And now good morrow to our waking souls,
   Which watch not one another out of fear;
For love, all love of other sights controls,
   And makes one little room, an everywhere.
Let sea-discoverers to new worlds have gone,
   Let maps to others, worlds on worlds have
      shown,
Let us possess our world, each hath one and
   is one.

My face in thine eye, thine in mine appears,
   And true plain hearts do in the faces rest,
Where can we find two better hemispheres
   Without sharp North, without declining West?
Whatever dies, was not mixed equally;
   If our two loves be one, or, thou and I
Love so alike, that none do slacken, none
   can die.

Ben Jonson (1572 – 1637)
Ben Jonson was born in London, the son of
a clergyman who died before Jonson's birth.
Jonson had the most varied career: bricklayer,
soldier and actor before becoming the most
influential writer of his day. A wild-tempered
(he killed two men in duels) but
warm-hearted man Jonson became the first
poet laureate in all but name in 1616 when
James I granted him a pension.

It is not growing like a tree
from **The underwood**
It is not growing like a tree
In bulk, doth make man better be;

Or standing long an oak, three hundred year,
To fall a log at last, dry, bald, and sere:
A lily of a day
Is fairer far, in May,
Although it fall and die that night;
It was the plant and flower of light.
In small proportions we just beauties see:
And in short measures life may perfect be.

To Celia

Drink to me only with thine eyes,
   And I will pledge with mine;
Or leave a kiss but in the cup
   And I'll not look for wine.
The thirst that from the soul doth rise
   Doth ask a drink divine;
But might I of Jove's nectar sup,
   I would not change for thine.
I sent thee late a rosy wreath,
   Not so much honouring thee
As giving it a hope that there
   It could not withered be;
But thou thereon didst only breathe,
   And sent'st it back to me;
Since when it grows, and smells, I swear,
   Not of itself but thee!

The shadow
(That women are but men's shadows)

Follow a shadow, it still flies you;
   Seem to fly it, it will pursue:
So court a mistress, she denies you;
   Let her alone, she will court you.
      Say, are not women truly, then,

13

Styled but the shadows of us men?
At morn and even, shades are longest;
   At noon they are or short or none:
So men at weakest, they are strongest,
   But grant us perfect, they're not known.
      Say, are not women truly, then,
      Styled but the shadows of us men?

Hymn to Diana

Queen and huntress, chaste and fair,
   Now the sun is laid to sleep,
Seated in thy silver chair
   State in wonted manner keep:
      Hesperus entreats thy light,
      Goddess excellently bright.

Earth, let not thy envious shade
   Dare itself to interpose;
Cynthia's shining orb was made
   Heaven to clear when day did close:
      Bless us then with wishèd sight,
      Goddess excellently bright.

Lay thy bow of pearl apart
   And thy crystal-shining quiver;
Give unto the flying hart
   Space to breathe, how short soever:
      Thou that mak'st a day of night,
      Goddess excellently bright!

George Herbert (1593 – 1633)

George Herbert was born in Wales in the late
sixteenth century into a life of deep religious
devotion. He was a deacon and a priest and

his poems, not surprisingly, are about the love of God, grace and salvation. But beyond their strictly devotional aspect, they derive much from the style of John Donne and were praised by Coleridge, who called them 'pure and unaffected'. Sadly for George Herbert, hardly any of his better poems were published in his lifetime, although in them he felt he had found the perfect expression for his love of all things divine.

Prayer

Prayer, the Church's banquet, Angel's age,
    God's breath in man returning to his birth,
The soul in paraphrase, heart in pilgrimage,
    The Christian plummet, sounding heaven and
      earth;

Engine against the Almighty, sinner's tower,
    Reversèd thunder, Christ-side-piercing spear,
The six-days' world transposing in an hour,
    A kind of tune, which all things hear and
      fear;

Softness and peace and joy, and love and bliss,
    Exalted manna, gladness of the best,
    Heaven in ordinary, man well drest,
The milky way, the bird of Paradise,

Church-bells beyond the stars heard, the soul's
    blood,
    The land of spices; something understood.

From **Man**
Man is all symmetry,
Full of proportions, one limb to another,
And all to all the world besides;
Each part may call the farthest brother,
For head with foot hath private amity,
And both with moons and tides.

Nothing hath got so far
But Man hath caught and kept it as his prey;
His eyes dismount the highest star;
He is in little all the sphere;
Herbs gladly cure our flesh, because that they
Find their acquaintance there.

For us the winds do blow,
The earth doth rest, heaven move and fountains
    flow,
Nothing we see but means our good,
As our delight or as our treasure;
The whole is either our cupboard of food
Or cabinet of pleasure.

The stars have us to bed,
Night draws the curtain, which the sun
    withdraws;
Music and light attend our head,
All things unto our flesh are kind
In their descent and being; to our mind
In their ascent and cause.

Each thing is full of duty
Waters united are our navigation;
Distinguishèd, our habitation;

16

Below, our drink; above, our meat;
Both are our cleanliness. Hath one such beauty?
Then how are all things neat!

More servants wait on Man
Than he'll take notice of: in every path
He treads down that which doth befriend him
When sickness makes him pale and wan.
Oh, mighty love! Man is one world, and hath
Another to attend him.

Since then, my God, Thou hast
So brave a palace built, O dwell in it,
That it may dwell with Thee at last!
Till then afford us so much wit,
That, as the world serves us, we may serve
   Thee,
And both thy servants be.

Discipline
Throw away thy rod,
Throw away thy wrath:
   O my God,
Take the gentle path.

For my heart's desire,
Unto thine is bent:
   I aspire
To a full consent.

Not a word or look
I affect to own,
   But by book,
And thy book alone.

Though I fail, I weep;
Though I halt in pace,
   Yet I creep
To the throne of grace.

Then let wrath remove;
Love will do the deed;
   For with love
Stony hearts will bleed.

Love is swift of foot,
Love's a man of war,
   And can shoot,
And can hit from far.

Who can 'scape his bow?
That which wrought on thee,
   Brought thee low,
Needs must work on me.

Throw away thy rod:
Though man frailties hath,
   Thou art God:
Throw away thy wrath.

Thomas Carew (1594/5 – 1640)
Carew was an officer at the court of
Charles I. His somewhat cynical verse made
him the most famous of the so-called
'Cavalier' poets. *On the Lady Mary Villiers is
a poignant remainder of our mortality.*

On the Lady Mary Villiers
The Lady Mary Villiers lies

Under this stone; with weeping eyes
The parents that first gave her birth,
And their sad friends, laid her in earth.
If any of them, Reader, were
Known unto thee, shed a tear;
Or if thyself possess a gem
As dear to thee, as this to them,
Though a stranger to this place,
Bewail in theirs thine own hard case:
  For thou perhaps at thy return
  Mayst find thy Darling in an urn.

John Milton(1608 – 74)

John Milton came close to being a driven
man. From his earliest years he believed that
something great was intended for him and he
fashioned his life to fulfil what he thought
would be expected of him. He immersed
himself in Latin because he saw it as a way of
becoming worthy of a divine destiny.

On a more practical level, he was a
republican, always keen to explain that, for
him, this meant a deep devotion to the cause
of liberty. That was why he pleaded the cause
of a free press to Parliament.

Milton was master of the grand, classical
style of English writing. His themes were of
epic greatness and human failure, of glory and
disgrace. The drama of Samson is finest of
all, a hero 'Eyeless in Gaza at the mill with
slaves': Milton's own blindness would have
enabled him to understand and to feel that
pain.

But it is a tribute to his skill that the work

is never deluged by self-serving pity or sentimentality. It moves with power and style from misery, dejection and a sense of hopelessness to humility and spiritual rebirth.

On his deceased wife
Methought I saw my late espoused Saint
    Brought to me like Alcestis from the grave,
    Whom Jove's great son to her glad husband gave,
    Rescued from death by force, though pale and faint.
Mine as whom washed from spot of child-bed taint,
    Purification in the old Law did save,
    And such, as yet once more I trust to have
    Full sight of her in Heaven without restraint,
Came vested all in white, pure as her mind:
    Her face was veiled, yet to my fancied sight,
    Love, sweetness, goodness, in her person shined
So clear, as in no face with more delight.
    But O as to embrace me she inclined
    I waked, she fled, and day brought back my night.

At a solemn music
Blest pair of sirens, pledges of heaven's joy,
Sphere-born harmonious sisters, Voice and Verse,
Wed your divine sounds, and mixed power employ
Dead things with inbreathed sense able to pierce,

And to our high-raised fantasy present
That indisturbed song of pure consent,
Aye sung before the sapphire-coloured throne
To him that sits thereon,
With saintly shout and solemn jubilee,
Where the bright Seraphim in burning row
Their loud uplifted angel-trumpets blow,
And the Cherubic host in thousand quires
Touch their immortal harps of golden wires,
With those just spirits that wear victorious
    palms,
Hymns devout and holy psalms
Singing everlastingly;
That we on earth with undiscording voice
May rightly answer that melodious noise:
As once we did, till disproportioned sin
Jarred against Nature's chime, and with harsh
    din
Broke the fair music that all creatures made
To their great Lord, whose love their motion
    swayed
In perfect diapson, whilst they stood
In first obedience and their state of good.
O may we soon again renew that song,
And keep in tune with heaven, till God ere
    long
To his celestial consort us unite,
To live with him, and sing in endless morn
    of light.

From **Samson Agonites**
O loss of sight, of thee I most complain!
Blind among enemies, O worse than chains,
Dungeon, or beggary, or decrepit age!

21

Light, the prime work of God, to me is
    extinct,
And all her various objects of delight
Annulled, which might in part my grief have
    eased,
Inferior to the vilest now become
Of man or worm, the vilest here excel me,
They creep, yet see, I dark in light exposed
To daily fraud, contempt, abuse and wrong,
Within doors, or without, still as a fool,
In power of others, never in my own;
Scarce half I seem to live, dead more than
    half.
O dark, dark, dark, amid the blaze of noon,
Irrecoverably dark, total eclipse,
Without all hope of day!
O first-created beam, and thou great Word,
'Let there be light, and light was over all,'
Why am I thus bereaved Thy prime decree?
The sun to me is dark
And silent as the moon,
When she deserts the night,
Hid in her vacant interlunar cave.
Since light so necessary is to life,
And almost life itself, if it be true
That light is in the soul,
She all in every part, why was the sight
To such a tender ball as the eye confined
So obvious and so easy to be quenched,
And not, as feeling, through all parts diffused,
That she might look at will through every
    pore?
Then had I not been thus exiled from light,
As in the land of darkness, yet in light,

To live a life half dead, a living death,
And buried; but, O yet more miserable!
Myself my sepulchre, a moving grave.

Abraham Cowley (1618 – 67)
Cowley was something of a child prodigy,
producing accomplished verse at the age of
ten. He was highly regarded in his day. On
his death, Charles II said that 'Mr Cowley
had not left a better man behind him in
England'. *Drinking* is his amusing celebration
of what was in Cromwell's England a vice.

Drinking
The thirsty earth soaks up the rain,
And drinks and gapes for drink again;
The plants suck in the earth, and are
With constant drinking fresh and fair;
The sea itself (which one would think
Should have but little need of drink)
Drinks ten thousand rivers up,
So filled that they o'erflow the cup.
The busy Sun (and one would guess
By's drunken fiery face no less)
Drinks up the sea, and when he's done,
The Moon and Stars drink up the Sun:
They drink and dance by their own light,
They drink and revel all the night:
Nothing in Nature's sober found,
But an eternal health goes round.
Fill up the bowl, then, fill it high,
Fill all the glasses there — for why
Should every creature drink but I?
Why, man of morals, tell me why?

Andrew Marvell (1621 – 78)
It is a great pity that in his lifetime and for
nearly 200 years after his death Andrew
Marvell was known more for his politics than
for his writing. He was MP for Hull for many
years and threw himself into being a House of
Commons man. He first opposed Cromwell,
but later became an admirer.

He was also passionate about writing. He
was a brilliant political satirist, and of that
school of seventeenth-century poets who wrote
on a wide variety of subjects both for pleasure
and for their friends. Most of his poetry was
published after his death by his housekeeper
who claimed to have been his wife.

To his coy mistress
Had we but world enough, and time,
This coyness, Lady, were no crime.
We would sit down, and think which way
To walk, and pass our long love's day.
Thou by the Indian Ganges side
Should'st rubies find: I by the tide
Of Humber would complain. I would
Love you ten years before the Flood,
And you should, if you please, refuse
Till the conversion of the Jews.
My vegetable love should grow
Vaster than empires, and more slow.
An hundred years should go to praise
Thine eyes, and on thy forehead gaze:
Two hundred to adore each breast;
But thirty thousand to the rest;
An age at least to every part,

And the last age should show your heart;
For, Lady, you deserve this state,
Nor would I love at lower rate,
   But at my back I always hear
Time's wingèd chariot hurrying near:
And yonder all before us lie
Deserts of vast eternity.
Thy beauty shall no more be found,
Nor, in thy marble vault, shall sound
My echoing song: then worms shall try
That long-preserved virginity,
And your quaint honour turn to dust
And into ashes all my lust:
The grave's a fine and private place,
But none, I think, do there embrace.
   Now, therefore, while the youthful hue
Sits on thy skin like morning dew,
And while thy willing soul transpires
At every pore with instant fires,
Now let us sport us while we may,
And now, like amorous birds of prey,
Rather at once our time devour,
Than languish in his slow-chapt power.
Let us roll all our strength and all
Our sweetness up into one ball,
And tear our pleasures with rough strife
Through the iron gates of life:
Thus, though we cannot make our sun
Stand still, yet we will make him run.

Bermudas

Where the remote Bermudas ride,
In the ocean's bosom unespied,
From a small boat, that rowed along,

The listening winds received this song.
    'What should we do but sing his praise,
That led us through the watery maze
Unto an isle so long unknown,
And yet far kinder than our own?
Where he the huge sea-monsters wracks,
That lift the deep upon their backs;
He lands us on a grassy stage,
Safe from the storms, and prelates' rage.
He gave us this eternal spring,
Which here enamels everything;
And sends the fowls to us in care,
On daily visits through the air.
He hangs in shades the orange bright,
Like golden lamps in a green night,
And does in the pomegranates close
Jewels more rich than Ormus shows.
He makes the figs our mouths to meet,
And throws the melons at our feet;
But apples plants of such a price
No tree could ever bear them twice.
With cedars, chosen by his hand,
From Lebanon, he stores the land;
And makes the hollow seas, that roar,
Proclaim the ambergris on shore.
He cast (of which we rather boast)
The Gospel's pearl upon our coast,
And in these rocks for us did frame
A temple, where to sound his Name.
Oh let our voice his praise exalt,
Till it arrive at heaven's vault,
Which thence (perhaps) rebounding, may
Echo beyond the Mexique Bay.'

Thus sung they in the English boat,
An holy and a cheerful note,
And all the way, to guide their chime,
With falling oars they kept the time.

The fair singer
To make a final conquest of all me,
Love did compose so sweet an enemy,
In whom both beauties to my death agree,
Joining themselves in fatal harmony;
That while she with her eyes my heart does
    bind,
She with her voice might captivate my mind.

I could have fled from one but singly fair:
My disentangled soul itself might save,
Breaking the curlèd trammels of her hair,
But how should I avoid to be her slave,
Whose subtle art invisibly can wreathe
My fetters of the very air I breathe?

It had been easy fighting in some plain,
Where victory might hang in equal choice;
But resistance against her is vain,
Who has the advantage both of eyes and voice;
And all my forces needs must be undone,
She having gainèd both the wind and sun.

The definition of love
My love is of a birth as rare
As 'tis for object strange and high:
It was begotten by despair
Upon impossibility.

27

Magnanimous despair alone
Could show me so divine a thing,
Where feeble hope could ne'er have flown
But vainly flapped its tinsel wing.

And yet I quickly might arrive
Where my extended soul is fixt,
But fate does iron wedges drive,
And always crowds itself betwixt.

For fate with jealous eye does see
Two perfect loves; nor lets them close:
Their union would her ruin be,
And her tyrannic power depose.

And therefore her decrees of steel
Us as the distant Poles have placed,
(Though love's whole world on us doth wheel)
Not by themselves to be embraced.

Unless the giddy Heaven fall,
And Earth some new convulsion tear;
And, us to join, the world should all
Be cramped into a planisphere.

As lines so loves oblique may well
Themselves in every angle greet:
But ours so truly parallel,
Though infinite, can never meet.

Therefore the love which us doth bind
But fate so enviously debars,
Is the conjunction of the mind,
And opposition of the stars.

Henry Carey (?1687 – 1743)

Carey wrote operas and farces, but his lasting fame is
due to the words and music of *Sally in our alley*.

Sally in our alley

Of all the girls that are so smart
   There's none like pretty Sally;
She is the darling of my heart,
   And she lives in our alley.
There is no lady in the land
   Is half so sweet as Sally;
She is the darling of my heart,
   And she lives in our alley.

Her father he makes cabbage-nets,
   And through the streets does cry 'em;
Her mother she sells laces long
   To such as please to buy 'em:
But sure such folks could ne'er beget
   So sweet a girl as Sally!
She is the darling of my heart,
   And she lives in our alley.

When she is by, I leave my work,
   I love her so sincerely;
My master comes like any Turk,
   And bangs me most severely:
But let him bang his bellyful,
   I'll bear it all for Sally;
She is the darling of my heart,
   And she lives in our alley.

Of all the days that's in the week
   I dearly love but one day —

And that's the day that comes betwixt
    A Saturday and Monday;
For then I'm drest all in my best
    To walk abroad with Sally;
She is the darling of my heart,
    And she lives in our alley.

My master carries me to church,
    And often am I blamed
Because I leave him in the lurch
    As soon as text is named;
I leave the church in sermon-time
    And slink away to Sally;
She is the darling of my heart,
    And she lives in our alley.

When Christmas comes about again,
    O, then I shall have money;
I'll hoard it up, and box and all
    I'll give it to my honey:
And would it were ten thousand pounds,
    I'd give it all to Sally,
She is the darling of my heart,
    And she lives in our alley.

My master and the neighbours all,
    Make game of me and Sally,
And, but for her, I'd better be
    A slave and row a galley;
But when my seven long years are out,
    O, then I'll marry Sally;
O, then we'll wed, and then we'll bed —
    But not in our alley!

Alexander Pope (1688 – 1744)

Pope's brilliance must have been unbearable to his contemporaries. He claimed to have taught himself Greek, French, and Italian at about the age of 12 and to have mastered Latin too. Much less in doubt is the fact that from these languages he drew his most famous aphorisms: 'A little learning is a dangerous thing', 'To err is human, to forgive divine', and even the seemingly more mundane, 'For fools rush in where angels fear to tread'. His *Elegy to the memory of an unfortunate lady* is a fine example of pathos and great beauty in verse:

So peaceful rests, without a stone, a name,
What once had beauty, titles, wealth and fame.

From An essay on criticism

A little learning is a dangerous thing;
Drink deep, or taste not the Pierian spring:
There shallow draughts intoxicate the brain,
And drinking largely sobers us again.
Fired at first sight with what the Muse imparts,
In fearless youth we tempt the heights of arts,
While from the bounded level of our mind,
Short views we take, nor see the lengths behind;
But more advanced, behold with strange surprise
New distant scenes of endless science rise!
So pleased at first the towering Alps we try,
Mount o'er the vales, and seem to tread the sky,
The eternal snows appear already passed,
And the first clouds and mountains seem the
    last:

But, those attained, we tremble to survey
The growing labours of the lengthened way,
The increasing prospect tires our wandering
  eyes,
Hills peep o'er hills, and Alps on Alps arise!
  A perfect judge will read each work of wit
With the same spirit that its author writ:
Survey the whole, nor seek slight faults to find
Where Nature moves, and rapture warms the
  mind,
Nor lose, for that malignant dull delight,
The generous pleasure to be charmeed with
  wit.
But in such lays as neither ebb nor flow,
Correctly cold, and regularly low,
That shunning faults, one quiet tenor keep;
We cannot blame indeed — but we may sleep.
In wit, as Nature, what affects our hearts
Is not the exactness of peculiar parts;
'Tis not a lip, or eye, we beauty call,
But the joint force and full result of all.
Thus when we view some well-proportioned
  dome
(The world's just wonder, and even thine, O
  Rome!)
No single parts unequally surprise,
All comes united to the admiring eyes;
No monstrous height, or breadth or length
  appear;
The whole at once is bold and regular.

Elegy to the memory of an unfortunate lady
  What beckoning ghost, along the moonlight
  shade

Invites my step, and points to yonder glade?
'Tis she! — But why that bleeding bosom
  gored,
Why dimly gleams the visionary sword?
Oh, ever beauteous, ever friendly! tell,
Is it, in Heaven, a crime to love too well?
To bear too tender, or too firm a heart,
To act a lover's or a Roman's part?
Is there no bright reversion in the sky
For those who greatly think, or bravely die?
    Why bade ye else, ye powers, her soul
  aspire
Above the vulgar flight of low desire?
Ambition first sprung from your blest abodes,
The glorious fault of angels and of gods;
Thence to their images on earth it flows,
And in the breasts of kings and heroes glows.
Most souls, 'tis true, but peep out once an
  age,
Dull sullen prisoners in the body's cage:
Dim lights of life, that burn a length of years
Useless, unseen, as lamps in sepulchres;
Like Eastern kings a lazy state they keep,
And close confined in their own palace sleep.
    From these perhaps (ere Nature bade her
  die)
Fate snatched her early to the pitying sky.
As into air the purer spirits flow,
And separate from their kindred dregs below;
So flew the soul to its congenial place,
Nor left one virtue to redeem her race.
    But thou, false guardian of a charge too
  good,
Thou, mean deserter of thy brother's blood!

33

See on these ruby lips the trembling breath,
These cheeks, now fading at the blast of death;
Cold is that breast which warmed the world
  before,
And those love-darting eyes must roll no more.
Thus, if eternal justice rules the ball,
Thus shall your wives, and thus your children
  fall:
On all the line a sudden vengeance waits,
And frequent hearses shall besiege your gates.
There passengers shall stand, and pointing say
(While the long funerals blacken all the way)
'Lo! these were they, whose souls the Furies
  steeled
And cursed with hearts unknowing how to
  yield.'
Thus unlamented, pass the proud away,
The gaze of fools, and pageant of a day!
So perish all whose breast ne'er learned to
  glow
For others' good, or melt at others' woe.
      What can atone (Oh ever injured shade!)
Thy fate unpitied, and thy rites unpaid?
No friend's complaint, no kind domestic tear
Pleased thy pale ghost, or graced thy mournful
  bier.
By foreign hands thy dying eyes were closed,
By foreign hands thy decent limbs composed,
By foreign hands thy humble grave adorned,
By strangers honoured, and by strangers mourned!
What though no friends in sable weeds appear,
Grieve for an hour, perhaps, then mourn a
  year,
And bear about the mockery of woe

34

To midnight dances, and the public show?
What, though no weeping loves thy ashes grace
Nor polished marble emulate thy face?
What though no sacred earth allow thee room,
Nor hallowed dirge be muttered o'er thy tomb?
Yet shall thy grave with rising flowers be
  dressed,
And the green turf lie lightly on thy breast
There shall the morn her earliest tears bestow,
There the first roses of the year shall blow;
While angels with their silver wings o'ershade
The ground, now sacred by thy relics made.
  So peaceful rests, without a stone, a name,
What once had beauty, titles, wealth and fame.
How loved, how honoured once, avails thee
  not,
To whom related, or by whom begot;
A heap of dust alone remains of thee:
'Tis all thou art, and all the proud shall be!
  Poets themselves must fall, like those they
  sung;
Deaf the praised ear, and mute the tuneful
  tongue.
Even he, whose soul now melts in mournful
  lays,
Shall shortly want the generous tear he pays;
Then from his closing eyes thy form shall part,
And the last pang shall tear thee from his
  heart;
Life's idle business at one gasp be o'er,
The Muse forgot, and thou beloved no more!

Ode on solitude
Happy the man, whose wish and care

A few paternal acres bound,
Content to breathe his native air
  In his own ground.

Whose herds with milk, whose fields with
    bread,
Whose flocks supply him with attire,
Whose trees in summer yield him shade,
  In winter fire.

Blest! who can unconcernedly find
Hours, days, and years slide soft away,
In health of body, peace of mind,
  Quiet by day.

Sound sleep by night; study and ease,
Together mixt; sweet recreation:
And innocence, which most does please
  With meditation.

Thus let me live, unseen, unknown,
Thus unlamented let me die,
Steal from the world, and not a stone
  Tell where I lie.

Thomas Gray (1716 – 71)
Thomas Gray was a rather reclusive and
unassuming man, but terribly learned for all
that, quite at home writing verse in Latin, and
in English. He spent many months polishing
his *Elegy*, and it brought him instant
recognition.

Dr Jonson praised its glorious images that
find 'a mirror in every mind', and Tennyson

commended its 'divine truisms'. Those truisms undoubtedly contributed to the poem's appeal. There is a universal truth about the poet's observation that regardless of pomp, power, beauty or wealth, 'The paths of glory lead but to the grave.'

Ode on the death of a favourite cat drowned in a tub of goldfishes
'Twas on a lofty vase's side,
   Where China's gaiest art had dyed
The azure flowers that blow;
Demurest of the tabby kind,
The pensive Selima reclined,
   Gazed on the lake below.

Her conscious tail her joy declared;
The fair round face, the snowy beard,
   The velvet of her paws,
Her coat that with the tortoise vies,
Her ears of jet and emerald eyes,
   She saw; and purred applause.

Still had she gazed; but 'midst the tide
Two angel forms were seen to glide,
   The Genii of the stream:
Their scaly armour's Tyrian hue
Through richest purple to the view
   Betrayed a golden gleam.

The hapless nymph with wonder saw:
A whisker first and then a claw,
   With many an ardent wish,
She stretched in vain to reach the prize.

What female heart can gold despise?
  What cat's averse to fish?

Presumptuous maid! with looks intent
Again she stretched, again she bent,
  Nor knew the gulf between.
(Malignant Fate sat by and smiled.)
The slippery verge her feet beguiled,
  She tumbled headlong in.

Eight times emerging from the flood
She mewed to every watery god,
  Some speedy aid to send.
No dolphin came, no Nereid stirred:
Nor cruel Tom nor Susan heard.
  A favourite has no friend!

From hence, ye beauties, undeceived,
Know, one false step is ne'er retrieved,
  And be with caution bold.
Not all that tempts your wandering eyes
And heedless hearts is lawful prize;
  Nor all that glisters gold.

From **Elegy written in a country churchyard**
The curfew tolls the knell of parting day,
The lowing herd winds slowly o'er the lea,
The ploughman homewards plods his weary
  way,
And leaves the world to darkness and to me.

Now fades the glimmering landscape on the
  sight,
And all the air a solemn stillness holds,

Save where the beetle wheels his droning flight,
And drowsy tinklings lull the distant folds;

Save that from yonder ivy-mantled tower
The moping owl does to the moon complain
Of such as, wandering near her secret bower,
Molest her ancient solitary reign.

Beneath those rugged elms, that yew-tree's
  shade
Where heaves the turf in many a mouldering
  heap,
Each in his narrow cell for ever laid
The rude forefathers of the hamlet sleep.

The breezy call of incense-breathing morn,
The swallow twittering from the straw-built
  shed,
The cock's shrill clarion, or the echoing horn,
No more shall rouse them from their lowly
  bed.

For them no more the blazing hearth shall
  burn
Or busy housewife ply her evening care;
No children run to lisp their sire's return,
Or climb his knees the envied kiss to share.

Oft did the harvest to their sickle yield,
Their furrow oft the stubborn glebe has broke;
How jocund did they drive their team afield!
How bowed the woods beneath their sturdy
  stroke!

Let not ambition mock their useful toil,
Their homely joys, and destiny obscure;
Nor grandeur hear with a disdainful smile
The short and simple annals of the poor.

The boast of heraldry, the pomp of power,
And all that beauty, all that wealth e'er gave,
Awaits alike the inevitable hour.
The paths of glory lead but to the grave.

Nor you, ye proud, impute to these the fault,
If memory o'er their tomb no trophies raise,
Where through the long-drawn aisle and fretted
    vault
The pealing anthem swells the note of praise.

Can storied urn or animated bust
Back to its mansion call the fleeting breath?
Can honour's voice provoke the silent dust,
Or flattery soothe the dull cold ear of death?

Oliver Goldsmith (?1730 – 74)
Oliver Goldsmith was one of the
brightest-shining lights of eighteenth-century
English literature. He wrote so widely and
with such brilliance that on his death his
friend Dr Jonson paid him the most
handsome tribute, saying that he 'left scarcely
any kind of writing untouched . . . and
touched nothing he did not adorn'. He
became very preoccupied about the spirit of
the age in which he lived. He saw a
coarsening in manners which he deplored and
he clearly felt that the expansionist dreams of

Empire were in the process of making England a less cultured and less civilised country. Here is an extract from *The deserted village*, a poem that deserves to be read in its entirety.

From **The deserted village**
Sweet smiling village, loveliest of the lawn,
  They sports are fled, and all thy charms
    withdrawn:
Amidst thy bowers the tyrant's hand is seen,
And desolation saddens all thy green:
One only master grasps the whole domain,
And half a tillage stints thy smiling plain:
No more thy glassy brook reflects the day,
But choked with sedges, works its weedy way.
Along thy glades, a solitary guest,
The hollow-sounding bittern guards its nest;
Amidst thy desert walks the lapwing flies,
And tires their echoes with unvaried cries.
Sunk are thy bowers in shapeless ruin all,
And the long grass o'ertops the mouldering
  wall;
And trembling, shrinking from the spoiler's
  hand,
Far, far away, thy children leave the land.
  Ill fares the land, to hastening ills a prey,
Where wealth accumulates, and men decay:
Princes and lords may flourish, or may fade;
A breath can make them, as a breath has
  made;
But a bold peasantry, their country's pride,
When once destroyed, can never be supplied.
  A time there was, ere England's griefs began,

When every rood of ground maintained its
    man;
For him light labour spread her wholesome
    store,
Just gave what life required, but gave no more:
His best companions, innocence and health;
And his best riches, ignorance of wealth.

But times are altered; trade's unfeeling train,
Usurp the land and dispossess the swain;
Along the lawn, where scattered hamlets rose,
Unwieldy wealth and cumbrous pomp repose;
And every want to luxury allied,
And every pang that folly pays to pride.
Those gentle hours that plenty bade to bloom,
Those calm desires that asked but little room,
Those healthful sports that graced the peaceful
    scene,
Lived in each look, and brightened all the green;
These, far departing, seek a kinder shore,
And rural mirth and manners are no more.

Song
When lovely woman stoops to folly,
    And finds too late that men betray,
What charm can sooth her melancholy,
    What art can wash her guilt away?

The only art her guilt to cover,
    To hide her shame from every eye,
To give repentance to her lover,
    And wring his bosom — is to die.

William Cowper (1731 – 1800)
William Cowper struggled with depression and

severe mental illness for much of his life, yet managed to write beautiful poetry and inspirational hymns. His main themes were ordinary people and everyday country life. He became something of a champion of the common man and, ignoring the complexities of the some of the literary styles of his time, he wrote with enviable clarity.

I learnt *The solitude of Alexander Selkirk*, with its very well-known opening lines, as a child at school, and had quite forgotten who wrote it. It has been wonderful to discover it again. Only the last stanza has been left out for reasons of space.

From **The solitude of Alexander Selkirk**
I am monarch of all I survey,
My right there is none to dispute;
From the centre all round to the sea
I am lord of the fowl and the brute.
O solitude! where are the charms
That sages have seen in thy face?
Better dwell in the midst of alarms
Than reign in this horrible place.

I am out of humanity's reach,
I must finish my journey alone,
Never hear the sweet music of speech;
I start at the sound of my own.
The beasts that roam over the plain
My form with indifference see;
They are so unacquainted with man,
Their tameness is shocking to me.

Society, friendship and love
Divinely bestowed upon man,
Oh, had I the wings of a dove
How soon would I taste you again!
My sorrows I then might assuage
In the ways of religion and truth,
Might learn from the wisdom of age,
And be cheered by the sallies of youth.

Ye winds that have made me your sport,
Convey to this desolate shore
Some cordial endearing report
Of a land I shall visit no more;
My friends, do they now and then send
A wish or a thought after me?
Oh tell me I yet have a friend,
Though a friend I am never to see.

How fleet is a glance of the mind!
Compared with the speed of its flight,
The tempest itself lags behind,
And the swift-wingèd arrows of light.
When I think of my own native land
In a moment I seem to be there;
But alas! recollection at hand
Soon hurries me back to despair.

The poplar field
The poplars are felled, farewell to the shade
And the whispering sound of the cool colonnade,
The winds play no longer, and sing in the
    leaves,
Nor Ouse on his bosom their image receives.

Twelve years have elapsed since I last took
    a view
Of my favourite field and the bank where they
    grew,
And now in the grass behold they are laid,
And the tree is my seat that once lent me a
    shade.

The blackbird has fled to another retreat
Where the hazels afford him a screen from
    the heat,
And the scene where his melody charmed me
    before,
Resounds with his sweet-flowing ditty no more.

My fugitive years are all hasting away,
And I must ere long lie as lowly as they,
With a turf on my breast, and a stone at
    my head,
Ere another such grove shall arise in its stead.

'Tis a sight to engage me, if anything can,
To muse on the perishing pleasures of man;
Though his life be a dream, his enjoyments, I see,
Have a being less durable even than he.

Light shining out of darkness
God moves in a mysterious way,
    His wonders to perform;
He plants his footsteps in the sea,
    And rides upon the storm.

Deep in unfathomable mines
    Of never failing skill

45

He treasures up his bright designs,
    And works his sovereign will.

Ye fearful saints, fresh courage take,
    The clouds ye so much dread
Are big with mercy, and shall break
    In blessings on your head.

Judge not the Lord by feeble sense,
    But trust him for his grace;
Behind a frowning providence,
    He hides a smiling face.

His purposes will ripen fast,
    Unfolding every hour;
The bud may have a bitter taste,
    But sweet will be the flower.

Blind unbelief is sure to err,
    And scan his work in vain;
God is his own interpreter,
    And he will make it plain.

William Blake (1757 – 1827)
Blake never went to school, but his skill as an
engraver opened the door to the world of
letters to him. The publication of *Songs of
innocence*, engraved by himself, in 1789, was
the finest of many self-illustrated volumes.
Blake was not much understood in his time
and Wordsworth's words were typical: 'There is
something in the madness in this man that
interests me more than the sanity
of Byron . . . ' Nevertheless, Blake became

one of the most influential poets in the language.

A poison tree

I was angry with my friend:
I told my wrath, my wrath did end.
I was angry with my foe:
I told it not, my wrath did grow.

And I watered it in fears,
Night and morning with my tears;
And I sunnèd it with smiles,
And with soft deceitful wiles.

And it grew by day and night,
Till it bore an apple bright;
And my foe beheld it shine,
And he knew that it was mine,

And into my garden stole
When the night had veiled the pole:
In the morning glad I see
My foe outstretched beneath the tree.

Auguries of innocence

To see a world in a Grain of Sand
And a Heaven in a Wild Flower,
Hold Infinity in the palm of your hand
And Eternity in an hour.

A Robin Redbreast in a Cage
Puts all Heaven in a Rage.
A dove-house filled with doves and pigeons
Shudders Hell through all its regions.

A dog starved at his Master's Gate
Predicts the ruin of the State.
A Horse misused upon the Road
Calls to Heaven for Human blood.
Each outcry from the hunted Hare
A fibre from the Brain does tear.
A Skylark wounded in the wing,
A Cherubim does cease to sing.
The Game Cock clipped and armed for fight
Does the Rising sun affright.
Every Wolf's and Lion's howl
Raises from Hell a Human Soul.
The wild deer, wandering here and there
Keeps the Human Soul from Care.
The Lamb Misused breeds Public strife,
And yet forgives the Butcher's Knife.
The Bat that flits at close of Eve
Has left the Brain that won't Believe.
The Owl that calls upon the Night
Speaks the Unbeliever's fright.
He who shall hurt the little Wren
Shall never be beloved by Men.
He who the Ox to wrath has moved
Shall never be by Woman loved.
The wanton Boy that kills the Fly
Shall feel the Spider's enmity.
He who torments the Chafer's sprite
Weaves a Bower in endless Night.
The Caterpillar on the Leaf
Repeats to thee thy Mother's grief.
Kill not the Moth nor Butterfly,
For the Last Judgement draweth nigh.
He who shall train the Horse to War
Shall never pass the Polar Bar.

The Beggar's Dog and Widow's Cat,
Feed them and thou wilt grow fat.
The Gnat that sings his Summer's song
Poison gets from Slander's tongue.
The poison of the Snake and Newt
Is the sweat of Envy's foot.
The Poison of the Honey Bee
Is the Artist's Jealousy.
The Prince's Robes and Beggar's Rags
Are Toadstools on the Miser's Bags.
A truth that's told with bad intent
Beats all the Lies you can invent.
It is right it should be so;
Man was made for Joy and Woe;
And when this we rightly know,
Through the World we safely go.
Joy and Woe are woven fine,
A Clothing for the Soul divine.
Under every grief and pine
Runs a joy with silken twine.
The Babe is more than swaddling Bands;
Throughout all these Human Lands.
Tools were made, and Born were hands,
Every Farmer Understands.
Every Tear from Every Eye
Becomes a Babe in Eternity;
This is caught by Females bright
And returned to its own delight.
The Bleat, the Bark, Bellow and Roar,
Are waves that Beat on Heaven's Shore.
The Babe that weeps the rod beneath
Write Revenge in realms of death.
The Beggar's Rags fluttering in Air
Does to Rags the Heavens tear.

The Soldier, armed with Sword and Gun
Palsied strikes the Summer's Sun.
The poor Man's Farthing is worth more
Than all the Gold on Afric's Shore.
One Mite wrung from the Labourer's hands
Shall buy and sell the Miser's Lands,
Or, if protected from on high,
Does that whole Nation sell and buy.
He who mocks the Infant's Faith
Shall be mocked in Age and Death.
He who shall teach the Child to Doubt
The rotting grave shall ne'er get out.
He who respects the Infant's Faith
Triumphs over Hell and Death.
The Child's Toys and the Old Man's Reasons
Are the Fruits of the Two seasons.
The Questioner, who sits so sly
Shall never know how to Reply.
He who replies to words of Doubt
Doth put the Light of Knowledge out.
The Strongest Poison ever known
Came from Caesar's Laurel Crown.
Nought can deform the Human Race
Like to the Armour's iron brace.
When Gold and Gems adorn the Plow,
To peaceful Hearts shall Envy Bow.
A Riddle, or the Cricket's Cry,
Is to Doubt a fit Reply.
The Emmet's inch and Eagle's Mile
Make Lame Philosophy to smile.
He who Doubts from what he sees
Will ne'er Believe, do what you Please.
If the Sun and Moon should doubt,
They'd immediately Go out.

To be in a Passion you Good may do,
But no Good if a Passion is in you.
The Whore and Gambler, by the State
Licensed, build that Nation's Fate.
The Harlot's cry from Street to Street.
Shall weave Old England's winding Sheet.
The Winner's Shout, the Loser's Curse,
Dance before dead England's Hearse.
Every Night and every Morn
Some to Misery are Born;
Every Morn and Every Night
Some are Born to sweet delight;
Some are Born to sweet delight,
Some are Born to Endless Night.
We are led to Believe a Lie
When we see not through the Eye
Which was Born in a Night to perish in Night
When the Soul Slept in Beams of Light.
God appears and God is Light
To those poor Souls who dwell in Night;
But does a Human Form Display
To those who Dwell in Realms of Day.

To the muses
Whether on Ida's shady brow,
Or in the chambers of the East,
The chambers of the sun, that now
From ancient melody have ceased;

Whether in Heaven ye wander fair,
Or the green corners of the earth,
Or the blue regions of the air,
Where the melodious winds have birth;

Whether on crystal rocks ye rove,
Beneath the bosom of the sea
Wandering in many a coral grove,
Fair Nine, forsaking Poetry!

How have you left the ancient love
That bards of old enjoyed in you!
The languid strings do scarcely move!
The sound is forced, the notes are few!

Piping down the valleys wild
Piping down the valleys wild,
Piping songs of pleasant glee,
On a cloud I saw a child,
And he laughing said to me:

'Pipe a song about a Lamb!'
So I piped with merry cheer.
'Piper, pipe that song again,'
So I piped: he wept to hear.

'Drop thy pipe, thy happy pipe,
Sing thy songs of happy cheer.'
So I sung the same again,
While he wept with joy to hear.

'Piper, sit thee down and write
In a book that all my read.'
So he vanished from my sight,
And I plucked a hollow reed,

And I made a rural pen,
And I stained the water clear,

And I wrote my happy songs
Every child may joy to hear.

The tiger
Tiger! Tiger! burning bright
In the forests of the night,
What immortal hand or eye
Could frame thy fearful symmetry?

In what distant deeps or skies
Burned the fire of thine eyes?
On what wings dare he aspire?
What the hand dare seize the fire?

And what shoulder, and what art,
Could twist the sinews of thy heart?
And when thy heart began to beat,
What dread hand? And what dread feet?

What the hammer? What the chain?
In what furnace was thy brain?
What the anvil? What dread grasp
Dare its deadly terrors clasp?

When the stars threw down their spears,
And watered heaven with their tears,
Did he smile his work to see?
Did he who made the Lamb make thee?

Tiger! Tiger! burning bright
In the forests of the night,
What immortal hand or eye
Dare frame thy fearful symmetry?

Robert Burns (1759 – 96)

The Scots are absolutely right to say that Robert Burns was a poetic genius. Equally unquestionable is the universality of his work. His poems and his ballads, many of which have been set to music, have captured the imagination of the world, and Burns the Scot has come close to being the voice of the people. The popularity of his work has never waned.

Burns wrote with emotion and wisdom, but always had the common touch. Most of all, so much of what he wrote is hauntingly beautiful. Sometimes the language is difficult, but not, I believe, in these poems.

Nothing said today can possibly enhance the reputation of Robert Burns. The fact that much of his poetry was written in Lowland Scottish vernacular denied many the pleasure and joy of his brilliance. But the esteem in which he is held acquired a truly international dimension. Burns left such a great body of work, that it is difficult to believe that when he died in 1796, he was only 37. The greater wisdom and insight he might have brought to his poetry and songs had he lived longer can only be guessed.

My love is like a red, red rose

O, my luve's like a red, red, rose,
That's newly sprung in June;
O, my luve's like the melodie
That's sweetly play'd in tune!

As fair art thou, my bonnie lass,
So deep in luve am I;
And I will luve thee still, my dear,
Till a' the seas gang dry:

Till a' the seas gang dry, my dear,
And the rocks melt wi' the sun;
I will luve thee still, my dear,
While the sands of life shall run.

And fare thee weel, my only luve!
And fare thee weel a while!
And I will come again, my luve,
Tho' it were ten thousand mile.

John Barleycorn
There was Three Kings into the east,
Three Kings both great and high,
And they hae sworn a solemn oath
John Barleycorn should die.

They took a plough and plough'd him down,
Put clods upon his head,
And they hae sworn a solemn oath
John Barleycorn was dead.

But the cheerfu' Spring came kindly on,
And show'rs began to fall;
John Barleycorn got up again,
And sore surprised them all.

The sultry suns of Summer came,
And he grew thick and strong,

His head weel arm'd wi' pointed spears,
That no one should him wrong.

The sober Autumn enter'd mild,
When he grew wan and pale;
His bending joints and drooping head
Show'd he'd begun to fail.

His colour sicken'd more and more,
He faded into age;
And then his enemies began
To shew their deadly rage.

They've ta'en weapon, long and sharp,
And cut him by the knee;
They tied him fast upon a cart,
Like a rogue for forgerie.

They laid him down upon his back,
And cudgell'd him full sore;
They hung him up before the storm,
And turn'd him o'er and o'er.

They filled up a darksome pit
With water to the brim,
They heaved in John Barleycorn,
They let him sink or swim.

They laid him out upon the floor,
To work him farther woe,
And still, as signs of life appear'd,
They toss'd him to and fro.

They wasted, o'er a scorching flame,
The marrow of his bones;
But a miller us'd him worst of all,
For he crush'd him between two stones.

And they hae ta'en his very heart's blood,
And drank it round and round;
And still the more and more they drank,
Their joy did more abound.

John Barleycorn was a hero bold,
Of noble enterprise,
For if you do but taste his blood,
'Twill make your courage rise.

'Twill make a man forget his woe;
'Twill heighten all his joy:
'Twill make the widow's heart to sing,
Tho' the tear were in her eye.

Then let us toast John Barleycorn,
Each man a glass in hand;
And may his great posterity
Ne'er fail in old Scotland!

From **The soldier's return**
When wild war's deadly blast was blawn,
And gentle Peace returning,
Wi' monie a sweet babe fatherless,
And monie a widow mourning:
I left the lines and tented field,
Where lang I'd been a lodger,
A humble knapsack a' my wealth,
A poor but honest sodger.

A leal, light heart was in my breast,
My hand unstain'd wi' plunder:
And for fair Scotia, hame again,
I cheery on did wander.
I thought upon the banks o'Coyl,
I thought upon my Nancy;
I thought upon the witching smile
That caught my youthful fancy.

At length I reached the bonny glen
Where early life I sported,
I passed the mill, and trysting-thorn,
Where Nancy aft I courted;
Wha spied I but my ain dear maid
Down by her mother's dwelling!
And turned me round to hide the flood
That in my een was swelling.

Wi' altered voice, quoth I, 'Sweet lass,
Sweet as yon hawthorn's blossom,
O happy, happy may he be,
That's dearest to thy bosom!
My purse is light, I've far to gang,
And fain would be thy lodger;
I've served my king and country lang —
Take pity on a sodger!'

Sae wistfully she gazed on me,
And lovelier was than ever;
Quo' she, 'A sodger ance I lo'ed,
Forget him I shall never:
Our humble cot, and hameley fare
Ye freely shall partake o't.'
That gallant badge, the dear cockade,

58

Ye're welcome for the sake o't.'

Sae flaxen were
Sae flaxen were her ringlets,
Her eyebrows of a darker hue,
Bewitchingly o'erarching
Twa laughing een o'bonnie blue.
Her smiling, sae wyling,
Wad make a wretch forget his woe;
What pleasure, what treasure,
Unto those rosy lips to grow!
Such was my Chloris' bonnie face,
When first her bonnie face I saw,
And aye my Chloris' dearest charm,
She says she lo'es me best of a'.

Like harmony her motion;
Her pretty ancle is a spy
Betraying fair proportion,
Wad make a saint forget the sky;
Sae warming, sae charming,
Her faultless form and gracefu' air;
Ilk feature — auld Nature
Declar'd that she could do nae mair:
Her are the willing chains o' love,
By conquering beauty's sovereign law;
And aye my Chloris' dearest charm,
She says she lo'es me best of a'.

Let others love the city,
And gaudy show at sunny noon;
Gie me the lonely valley,
The dewy eve, and rising moon
Fair beaming, and streaming

59

Her silver light the boughs amang;
While falling, recalling,
The amorous thrush concludes his sang,
There, dearest Chloris, wilt thou rove
By wimling burn and leafy shaw,
And hear my vows o' truth and love,
And say thou lo'es me best of a'?

William Wordsworth (1770 – 1850)

William Wordsworth was a consummate poet
and the leading influence in that great English
Romantic Movement of the late eighteenth
and early nineteenth centuries — a time that
produced work of ravishing beauty.
Wordsworth blossomed through his association
with Samuel Taylor Coleridge, and lavished
his skill on lyrical descriptions of life and the
English countryside. But his canvas was
broader. Enchanted by the passions of the
French Revolution he penned the memorable
lines: 'Bliss was it in that dawn to be alive,/
But to be young was very Heaven!' His sister
Dorothy devoted her life to him and to the
nurturing of his art; *The solitary reaper* was
written after a walk with her.

I have always considered these lines from
Tintern Abbey as being the most gloriously
descriptive of anything William Wordsworth
wrote. The beauty is irresistible. They convey
an overpowering sense of nostalgia, recalling
memories of 'sensations sweet, felt in the
blood and felt along the heart'. They light up
the mind and inspire thoughts of all that's
finest about our existence.

From **Tintern Abbey**

These beauteous forms,
Through a long absence, have not been to me
As is a landscape to a blind man's eye:
But oft, in lonely rooms, and 'mid the din
Of towns and cities, I have owed to them,
In hours of weariness, sensations sweet,
Felt in the blood, and felt along the heart;
And passing even into my purer mind,
With tranquil restoration: feelings too
Of unremembered pleasure: such, perhaps,
As have no slight or trivial influence
On that best portion of a good man's life,
His little, nameless, unremembered, acts
Of kindness and of love. Nor less, I trust,
To them I may have owed another gift,
Of aspect more sublime; that blessed mood,
In which the burthen of the mystery,
In which the heavy and the weary weight
Of all this unintelligible world,
Is lightened: that serene and blessed mood,
In which the affections gently lead us on,
Until, the breath of this corporeal frame
And even the motion of our human blood
Almost suspended, we are laid asleep
In body, and become a living soul:
While with an eye made quiet by the power
Of harmony, and the deep power of joy,
We see into the life of things.
　　If this
Be but a vain belief, yet, oh! how oft —
In darkness and amid the many shapes
Of joyless daylight; when the fretful stir
Unprofitable, and the fever of the world,

Have hung upon the beatings of my heart —
How oft, in spirit, have I turned to thee,
O sylvan Wye! thou wanderer through the woods,
How often has my spirit turned to thee!

Nutting

It seems a day
(I speak of one from many singled out),
One of those heavenly days which cannot die,
When forth I sallied from our cottage-door,
And with a wallet o'er my shoulder slung,
A nutting crook in hand, I turned my steps
Towards the distant woods, a figure quaint,
Tricked out in proud disguise of beggar's weeds
Put on for the occasion, by advice
And exhortation of my frugal Dame.
Motley accoutrement! of power to smile
At thorns, and brakes, and brambles, and, in truth,
More ragged than need was. Among the woods,
And o'er the pathless rocks, I forced my way
Until, at length, I came to one dear nook
Unvisited, where not a broken bough
Drooped with its withered leaves (ungracious
    sign
Of devastation), but the hazels rose
Tall and erect, with white-milk clusters hung —
A virgin scene! A little while I stood,
Breathing with such suppression of the heart
As joy delights in, and with wise restraint
Voluptuous, fearless of a rival, eyed
The banquet, or beneath the trees I sat
Among the flowers, and with the flowers I
played:

62

A temper known to those, who, after long
And weary expectation, have been blessed
With sudden happiness beyond all hope.
Perhaps it was a bower beneath whose leaves
The violets of five seasons re-appear
And fade, unseen by any human eye,
Where fairy water-breaks do murmur on
For ever, and I saw the sparkling foam,
And with my cheek on one of those green
   stones
That, fleeced with moss, beneath the shady
   trees,
Lay round me scattered like a flock of sheep,
I heard the murmur and the murmuring sound,
In that sweet mood when pleasure loves to pay
Tribute to ease, and, of its joy secure,
The heart luxuriates with indifferent things,
Wasting its kindliness on stocks and stones,
And on the vacant air. Then up I rose,
And dragged to earth both branch and bough,
   with crash
And merciless ravage, and the shady nook
Of hazels, and the green and mossy bower
Deformed and sullied, patiently gave up
Their quiet being: and unless I now
Confound my present feelings with the past,
Even then, when from the bower I turned away,
Exulting, rich beyond the wealth of kings,
I felt a sense of pain when I beheld
The silent trees and the intruding sky.

Then, dearest maiden! move along these shades
In gentleness of heart; with gentle hand
Touch — for there is a spirit in the woods.

From **French Revolution**
Oh pleasant exercise of hope and joy!
For mighty were the auxiliars which then stood
Upon our side, we who were strong in love!
Bliss was it in that dawn to be alive,
But to be young was very heaven! — Oh! times
In which the meagre, stale, forbidding ways
Of custom, law, and statute, took at once
The attraction of a country in romance!
When Reason seemed the most to assert her
  rights,
When most intent on making of herself
A prime Enchantress — to assist the work
Which then was going forward in her name!
Not favoured spots alone, but the whole earth,
The beauty wore of promise, that which sets
(As at some moment might not be unfelt
Among the bowers of paradise itself)
The budding rose above the rose full blown.
What temper at the prospect did not wake
To happiness unthought of? The inert
Were roused, and lively natures rapt away!
They who had fed their childhood upon dreams,
The playfellows of fancy, who had made
All powers of swiftness, subtlety, and strength
Their ministers — who in lordly wise had
  stirred
Among the grandest objects of the sense,
And dealt with whatsoever they found there
As if they had within some lurking right
To wield it.

The solitary reaper
Behold her, single in the field,

64

Yon solitary Highland lass!
Reaping and singing by herself;
　Stop here, or gently pass!
Alone she cuts and binds the grain,
And sings a melancholy strain;
O listen! for the vale profound
Is overflowing with the sound.

No nightingale did ever chant
　More welcome notes to weary bands
Of travellers in some shady haunt,
　Among Arabian sands:
A voice so thrilling ne'er was heard
In spring-time from the cuckoo bird,
Breaking the silence of the seas
Among the farthest Hebrides.

Will no one tell me what she sings? —
　Perhaps the plaintive numbers flow
For old, unhappy far-off things,
　And battles long ago:
Or is it some more humble lay,
Familiar matter of today?
Some natural sorrow, loss or pain,
That has been, and may be again?

Whate'er the theme, the maiden sang
　As if her song could have no ending;
I saw her singing at her work,
　And o'er the sickle bending; —
I listened, motionless and still;
And, as I mounted up the hill,
The music in my heart I bore,
Long after it was heard no more.

Upon Westminster Bridge, September 3, 1802

Earth has not anything to show more fair:
  Dull would he be of soul who could pass by
  A sight so touching in its majesty:
This City now doth, like a garment, wear
The beauty of the morning; silent, bare,
  Ships, towers, domes, theatres, and temples lie
  Open unto the fields, and to the sky;
All bright and glittering in the smokeless air.
Never did sun more beautifully steep
  In his first splendour, valley, rock or hill;
Ne'er I saw I, never felt, a calm so deep!
  The river glideth at his own sweet will:
Dear God! the very houses seem asleep;
  And all that mighty heart is lying still!

Sir Walter Scott (1771 – 1832)

Walter Scott was born in Edinburgh towards the end of the eighteenth century, and was passionate about the Borders from where his family came. He wrote descriptive ballads about the area, and immersed himself in its romantic tales and folklore. *The lay of the last minstrel* was the long poem that brought his work to public attention. It is based on a Border narrative, and supposedly recited by an old minstrel to the Duchess of Buccleuch and her ladies in Newark Castle. Scott's ability to tell these stories vividly, and with drama and style, made him a significant contributor to Scottish literature. *The lay of the last minstrel*, from which *Patriotism* is the Sixth Canto, deserves to be read at length.

Patriotism (Innominatus)

Breathes there the man, with soul so dead,
Who never to himself hath said,
  This is my own, my native land!
Whose heart hath ne'er within him burn'd
As home his footsteps he hath turn'd,
  From wandering on a foreign strand!
If such there breathe, go, mark him well;
For him no Minstrel raptures swell:
High though his titles, proud his name,
Boundless his wealth as wish can claim;
Despite those titles, power and pelf,
The wretch, concentred all in self,
Living, shall forfeit fair renown,
And doubly dying, shall go down
To the vile dust, from whence he sprung,
Unwept, unhonour'd, and unsung.

O Caledonia! stern and wild,
Meet nurse for a poetic child!
Land of brown heath and shaggy wood,
Land of the mountain and the flood,
Land of my sires! what mortal hand
Can e'er untie the filial band,
That knits me to thy rugged strand!
Still, as I view each well-known scene,
Think what is now, and what hath been,
Seems as, to me, of all bereft,
Sole friends thy woods and streams were left;
And thus I love them better still,
Even in extremity of ill.
By Yarrow's streams still let me stray,
Though none should guide my feeble way;
Still feel the breeze down Ettrick break;

Although it chill my wither'd cheek;
Still lay my head by Teviot Stone,
Though there, forgotten and alone,
The Bard may draw his parting groan.

The rover's farewell

A weary lot is thine, fair maid,
  A weary lot is thine!
To pull the thorn thy brow to braid,
  And press the rue for wine.
A lightsome eye, a soldier's mien,
  A feather of the blue,
A doublet of the Lincoln green —
  No more of me you knew,
    My Love!
No more of me you knew.

'This morn is merry June, I trow,
  The rose is budding fain;
But she shall bloom in winter snow
  Ere we two meet again.'
— He turned his charger as he spake
  Upon the river shore,
He gave his bridle-reins a shake,
  Said 'Adieu for evermore,
    My Love!
And adieu for evermore.'

An hour with thee

An hour with thee! When earliest day
Dapples with gold the eastern grey,
Oh, what can frame my mind to bear
The toil and turmoil, cark and care,
New griefs, which coming hours unfold,

And sad remembrance of the old?
  One hour with thee.

One hour with thee! When burning June
Waves his red flag at pitch of noon;
What shall repay the faithful swain,
His labour on the sultry plain;
And, more than cave or sheltering bough?
Cool feverish blood and throbbing brow?
  One hour with thee.

One hour with thee! When sun is set,
Oh, what can teach me to forget
The thankless labours of the day;
The hopes, the wishes, flung away;
The increasing wants, and lessening gains,
The master's pride, who scorns my pains?
  One hour with thee.

Lochinvar

O, young Lochinvar is come out of the west,
Through all the wide Border his steed was
    the best;
And save his good broadsword he weapons
    had none,
He rode all unarmed, and he rode all alone.
So faithful in love, and so dauntless in war,
There never was knight like the young Lochinvar.

He stayed not for brake, and he stopped not for
    stone,
He swam the Eske river where ford there was
    none;
But ere he alighted at Netherby gate,

The bride had consented, the gallant came
late:
For a laggard in love, and a dastard in war,
Was to wed the fair Ellen of brave Lochinvar.
So boldly he entered the Netherby Hall,
Among the bride's-men, and kinsmen, and
brothers, and all:
Then spoke the bride's father, his hand on his
sword,
(For the poor craven bridegroom said never a
word)
'O come ye in peace here, or come ye in war,
Or to dance at our bridal, young Lord
Lochinvar?'

'I long wooed your daughter, my suit you
denied; —
Love swells like the Solway, but ebbs like its
tide —
And now am I come, with this lost love of
mine,
To lead but one measure, drink one cup of
wine.
There are maidens in Scotland more lovely
by far,
That would gladly be bride to the young
Lochinvar.'
The bride kissed the goblet: the knight took
it up,
He quaffed off the wine, and he threw down
the cup.
She looked down to blush, and she looked up
to sigh,
With a smile on her lips, and a tear in her eye.

He took her soft hand, ere her mother could
  bar, —
'Now we tread a measure!' said the young
  Lochinvar.

So stately his form and so lovely her face,
That never a hall such a galliard did grace;
While her mother did fret, and her father did
  fume,
And the bridegroom stood dangling his bonnet
  and plume;
And the bride-maidens whispered ' 'Twere better
  by far,
To have matched our fair cousin with young
  Lochinvar.'

One touch to her hand, and one word in
  her ear,
When they reached the hall-door, and the
  charger stood near;
So light to the croup the fair lady he swung,
So light to the saddle before her he sprung!
'She is won! we are gone, over bank, bush and
  scaur;
They'll have fleet steeds that follow,' quoth
  young Lochinvar.

There was mounting 'mong Graemes of the
  Netherby clan;
Forsters, Fenwicks, and Musgraves, they rode
  and they ran:
There was racing and chasing on Cannobie Lee,
But the lost bride of Netherby ne'er did they
  see.

So daring in love, and so dauntless in war,
Have ye e'er heard of gallant like young
Lochinvar?

Lord Byron (1788 – 1824)
Byron is supreme among English poets. So
colourful was his life, and so sensational were
his love affairs, that for a time the man
seemed a greater focus for scholarly study
than the poet. But this soon changed, and
despite the personal scandals in which he was
almost continuouly involved, his brilliance
illuminated the world of poetry as no other.
He was acknowledged as a master of his art
even when he found himself ostracised by
English society. He was particularly proud of
his verse dramas, of which *Manfred*, the
outcast, was one. Byron lived his life to the
full, and died tragically early. The passion,
power and beauty of his work live on
gloriously.

She walks in beauty
She walks in beauty, like the night
　Of cloudless climes and starry skies;
And all that's best of dark and bright
　Meet in her aspect and her eyes:
Thus mellowed to that tender light
　Which heaven to gaudy day denies.

One shade the more, one ray the less,
　Had half impaired the nameless grace
Which waves in every raven tress,
　Or softly lightens o'er her face

Where thoughts serenely sweet express
    How pure, how dear their dwelling place.

And on that cheek and o'er that brow
    So soft, so calm, yet eloquent,
The smiles that win, the tints that glow,
    But tell of days in goodness spent,
A mind at peace with all below,
    A heart whose love is innocent.

The incantation (*from* Manfred)
When the moon is on the wave,
And the glow-worm in the grass,
And the meteor on the grave,
And the wisp on the morass;
When the falling stars are shooting,
And the answered owls are hooting,
And the silent leaves are still
In the shadow of the hill,
Shall my soul be upon thine,
With a power and a sign.

Though thy slumber may be deep,
Yet thy spirit shall not sleep;
There are shades which will not vanish,
There are thoughts thou canst not banish;
By a power to thee unknown,
Thou canst never be alone;
Thou art wrapt as with a shroud,
Thou art gathered in a cloud;
And for ever shalt thou dwell
In the spirit of this spell.

Though thou seest me not pass by,
Thou shalt feel me with thine eye
As a thing that, though unseen,
Must be near thee, and hath been;
And when in that secret dread
Thou has turned around thy head,
Thou shalt marvel I am not
As thy shadow on the spot,
And the power which thou dost feel
Shall be what thou must conceal.

And a magic voice and verse
Hath baptized thee with a curse;
And a spirit of the air
Hath begirt thee with a snare;
In the wind there is a voice
Shall forbid thee to rejoice;
And to thee shall night deny
All the quiet of her sky;
And the day shall have a sun,
Which shall make thee wish it done.

So, we'll go no more a-roving
So, we'll go no more a-roving
   So late into the night,
Though the heart be still as loving,
   And the moon be still as bright.

For the sword outwears its sheath,
   And the soul wears out the breast,
And the heart must pause to breathe,
   And love itself have rest.

Though the night was made for loving,
  And the day returns too soon,
Yet we'll go no more a-roving
  By the light of the moon.

Charles Wolfe (1791 – 1823)
The burial of Sir John Moore at Corunna is
one of those poems I learnt in primary school
and never forgot. Even at that tender age, I
remember that it began to inspire in me a less
than glamorous view of war. The poem makes
its point with deep poignancy. It is dedicated,
in a way, to showing up the human cost of
many celebrated conflicts. Sir John Moore, who
clearly deserved better, does not even have the
benefit of a decent burial, nor is his place of
rest marked out in any special way for fear
that it may be desecrated. In any event, his
comrades in arms, anxious to keep ahead of
the 'distant and random gun/ That the foe was
sullenly firing' decided to leave him alone in
his glory. There is now, however, a handsome
memorial at Corunna to Sir John Moore.

The burial of Sir John Moore at Corunna
Not a drum was heard, not a funeral note,
  As his corpse to the rampart we hurried;
Not a soldier discharged his farewell shot
  O'er the grave where our hero we buried.

We buried him darkly at dead of night,
  The sods with our bayonets turning,
By the struggling moonbeam's misty light
  And the lanthorn dimly burning.

No useless coffin enclosed his breast,
  Not in sheet or in shroud we wound him;
But he lay like a warrior taking his rest
  With his martial cloak around him.

Few and short were the prayers we said,
  And we spoke not a word of sorrow;
But we steadfastly gazed on the face that was dead,
  And we bitterly thought of the morrow.

We thought, as we hollowed his narrow bed
  And smoothed down his lonely pillow,
That the foe and the stranger would tread o'er his head,
  And we far away on the billow!

Lightly they'll talk of the spirit that's gone
  And o'er his cold ashes upbraid him —
But little he'll reck, if they let him sleep on
  In the grave where a Briton has laid him.

But half of our heavy task was done
  When the clock struck the hour for retiring;
And we heard the distant and random gun
  That the foe was sullenly firing.

Slowly and sadly we laid him down,
  From the field of his fame fresh and gory;
We carved not a line and we raised not a stone,
  But we left him alone with his glory.

Percy Bysshe Shelley (1792 – 1822)
In his short life, Shelley aroused vastly

different and contradictory emotions. To some contemporaries he was 'a base bad man . . . the vilest wretch'. To his friends he was 'gentle, generous, accomplished and brave'. His relationship with a number of women left much to be desired and incurred virulent criticism. What is not in doubt is the lyrical majesty of his work. He is the most romantic of poets. The language is boundless with emotion: 'Trembles and sparkles as with ecstasy,/ Possessing and possessed by all that is/ Within that calm circumference of bliss . . . ' Needless to say the most magnificent of love poems, *Epipsychidion*, was addressed to one of his ladies, Emilia Viviani.

Similes for two political characters of 1819
As from an ancestral oak
Two empty ravens sound their clarion,
Yell by yell, and croak by croak,
When they scent the noonday smoke
Of fresh human carrion:

As two gibbering night-birds flit,
From their bowers of deadly hue
Through the night to frighten it,
When the moon is in a fit,
And the stars are none or few:

As a shark and dogfish wait
Under an Atlantic isle,
For the negro-ship, whose freight
Is the theme of their debate,
Wrinkling their red gills the while

77

Are ye, two vultures sick for battle,
Two scorpions under one wet stone,
Two bloodless wolves whose dry throats rattle,
Two crows perched on the murrained cattle,
Two vipers tangled into one.

Love's philosophy

The fountains mingle with the river
    And the rivers with the ocean,
The winds of heaven mix for ever
    With a sweet emotion;
Nothing in the world is single;
    All things by a law divine
In one spirit meet and mingle.
    Why not I with thine? —

See the mountain kiss high heaven
    And the waves clasp one another;
No sister flower would be forgiven
    If it disdained its brother;
And the sunlight clasps the earth
    And the moonbeams kiss the sea:
What is all this sweet work worth
    If thou kiss not me?

Ozymandias

I met a traveller from an antique land
Who said: Two vast and trunkless legs of stone
Stand in the desert. Near them on the sand,
Half sunk, a shattered visage lies, whose frown,
And wrinkled lip and sneer of cold command,
Tell that its sculptor well those passions read
Which yet survive, stamped on these lifeless
    things,

The hand that mocked them, and the hand
   that fed;
And on the pedestal these words appear:
'My name is Ozymandias, king of kings:
Look on my works, ye Mighty and despair!'
Nothing beside remains. Round the decay
Of that colossal wreck, boundless and bare,
The lone and level sands stretch far away.

From **Epipsychidion**
This isle and house are mine, and I have
   vowed
Thee to be a lady of the solitude.
And I have fitted up some chambers there
Looking towards the golden Eastern air,
And level with the living winds, which flow
Like waves above the living waves below.
I have sent books and music there, and all
Those instruments with which high spirits call
The future from its cradle, and the past
Out of its grave, and make the present last
In thoughts and joys which sleep, but cannot
   die,
Folded within their own eternity.
Our simple life wants little, and true taste
Hires not the pale drudge Luxury to waste
The scene it would adorn, and therefore still,
Nature with all her children, haunts the hill.
The ringdove, in the embowering ivy, yet
Keeps up her love-lament, and the owls flit
Round the evening tower, and the young stars
   glance
Between the quick bats in their twilight dance;
The spotted deer bask in the fresh moonlight

Before our gate, and the slow silent night
Is measured by the pants of their calm sleep.
Be this our home in life, and when years heap
Their withered hours, like leaves, on our decay,
Let us become the overhanging day,
The living soul of this Elysian isle,
Conscious, inseparable, one. Meanwhile
We two will rise, and sit, and walk together,
Under the roof of blue Ionian weather,
And wander in the meadows, or ascend
The mossy mountains, where the blue heavens
    bend
With lightest winds, to touch their paramour;
Or linger, where the pebble-paven shore,
Under the quick faint kisses of the sea
Trembles and sparkles as with ecstasy,
Possessing and possessed by all that is
Within that calm circumference of bliss,
And by each other, till to love and live
Be one.

John Clare (1793 – 1864)

John Clare's life was deeply stained by
tragedy, but is a fine example of what can be
achieved from unpromising beginnings. Clare
was born into a farming family, left school at
11 and spent his early years working in the
fields. Neither his immediate family nor other
people in the community looked far beyond
their immediate surroundings. But Clare had
a vision of what he wanted his life to be and,
having educated himself, he began secretly
writing poetry. He wrote about nature, the
countryside and the changing seasons and

achieved acclaim briefly in the 1820s. But he spent the last 20 years of his life locked in an asylum. That his work survives today is a tribute to its originality and its haunting beauty.

With garments flowing

Come, come, my love, the bush is growing.
   The linnet sings the tune again
He sung when thou with garments flowing
   Went talking with me down the lane.
Dreaming of beauty, ere I found thee,
   And musing by the bushes green;
The wind, enamoured, streaming round thee
   Painted the visions I had seen.

I guessed thy face without the knowing
   Was so beautiful as e'er was seen;
I thought so by the garments flowing
   And gait as airy as a queen;
Thy shape, thy size, could not deceive me:
   Beauty seemed hid in every limb;
And then thy face, when seen, believe me,
   Made every former fancy dim.

Yes, when thy face in beauty brightened
   The music of a voice divine,
Upon my heart thy sweetness lightened;
   Life, love, that moment, all were thine;
All I imagined musing lonely,
   When dreaming 'neath the greenwood tree,
Seeming to fancy visions only,
   Breathed living when I met with thee.

I wander oft, not to forget thee
　　But just to feel those joys again.
When by the hawbush stile I met thee
　　And heard thy voice adown the lane
Return me its good-humoured greeting:
　　And oh! what music met my ear!
And then thy looks of wonder meeting,
　　To see me come and talk so near!

Thy face that held no sort of scorning,
　　Thy careless jump to reach the may;
That bush — I saw it many a morning
　　And hoped to meet thee many a day;
Till winter came and stripped the bushes,
　　The thistle withered on the moors,
Hopes sighed like winds along the rushes —
　　I could not meet thee out of doors.

But winter's gone and spring is going
　　And by thy own fireside I've been,
And told thee, dear, with garments flowing
　　I met thee when the spring was green;
When travellers through snow-deserts rustle,
　　Far from the strife of humankind,
How little seems the noise and bustle
　　Of places they have left behind!

And on that long-remembered morning
　　When first I lost this heart of mine,
Fame, all I'd hoped for, turned to scorning
　　And love, and hope lived wholly thine;
I told thee and with rapture glowing
　　I heard thee more than once declare,
That down the lane with garments flowing

Thou with the spring wouldst wander
there.

Song: I hid my love
I hid my love when young till I
Couldn't bear the buzzing of a fly;
I hid my love to my despite
Till I could not bear to look at light:
I dare not gaze upon her face
But left her memory in each place;
Where'er I saw a wild flower lie
I kissed and bade my love goodbye.

I met her in the greenest dells,
Where dewdrops pearl the wood bluebells;
The lost breeze kissed her bright blue eye,
The bee kissed and went singing by,
A sunbeam found a passage there,
A gold chain round her neck so fair;
As secret as the wild bee's song
She lay there all the summer long.

I hid my love in field and town
Till e'en the breeze would knock me down;
The bees seemed singing ballads o'er,
The fly's bass turned a lion's roar;
And even silence found a tongue,
To haunt me all the summer long;
The riddle nature could not prove
Was nothing else but secret love.

The request
Now the sun his blinking beam
Behind yon mountain loses,

And each eye, that might evil deem,
In blinded slumber closes:
Now the field's a desert grown,
Now the hedger's fled the grove,
Put thou on thy russet gown,
Shielded from the dews, my love,
And wander out with me.

We have met at early day,
Slander rises early,
Slander's tongues had much to say,
And still I love thee dearly:
Slander now to rest has gone,
Only wakes the courting dove;
Slyly steal thy bonnet on,
Leave thy father's cot, my love,
And wander out with me.

Clowns have passed our noonday screen,
'Neath the hawthorn's blossom,
Seldom there the chance has been
To press thee to my bosom:
Ploughmen now no more appear,
Night-winds but the thorn-bough move;
Squander not a minute here,
Lift the door-latch gently, love,
And wander out with me.

Oh the hour so sweet as this,
With friendly night surrounded,
Left free to talk, embrace, and kiss,
By virtue only bounded
Lose it not, make no delay,
Put on thy doublet, hat, and glove,

Sly ope the door and steal away;
And sweet 'twill be, my only love,
To wander out with thee.

Hares at play
The birds are gone to bed, the cows are still
And sheep lie panting on each old molehill
And underneath the willow's grey-green bough
Like toil a-resting, lies the fallow plough.
The timid hares throw daylight's fears away
On the lane's road to dust and dance and play
Then dabble in the grain by nought deterred
To lick the dewfall from the barley's beard
Then out they sturt again and round the hill
Like happy thoughts dance, squat and loiter
    still
Till milking maidens in the early morn
Jingle their yokes and start them in the corn
Through well-known beaten paths each nimbling
    hare
Sturts quick as fear — and seeks its hidden
    lair.

John Keats (1795 – 1821)
Tragedy is such an inescapable dimension of
Keats's life that it is sometimes very difficult
to regard him as the most brilliant poet. He
achieved that status by sheer determination.
For him it was very close to being a call of
destiny. Thus, when his work was dismissed
and derided by others, many of whom were
far less gifted, he dug his toes in, worked
harder at his art and against the conventional
wisdom of the time, prophesied: 'I think I

shall be among the English poets after my death.' He wrote about joy and sorrow, life and death. 'The excellence of every Art', he said, 'is in its intensity, capable of making all disagreeables evaporate.'

La belle dame sans merci

'O what can ail thee, knight-at-arms,
    Alone and palely loitering?
The sedge is withered from the lake,
    And no birds sing.

'O, what can ail thee, knight-at-arms,
    So haggard and so woebegone?
The squirrel's granary is full,
    And the harvest's done.

'I see a lily on thy brow,
    With anguish moist and fever-dew,
And on thy cheeks a fading rose
    Fast withereth too.

'I met a lady in the meads,
    Full beautiful — a faery's child,
Her hair was long, her foot was light,
    And her eyes were wild.

'I made a garland for her head,
    And bracelets too, and fragrant zone;
She looked at me as she did love,
    And made sweet moan.

'I set her on my pacing steed
    And nothing else saw all day long;

For sideways she would lean, and sing
  A faery's song.

'She found me roots of relish sweet,
  And honey wild and manna dew,
And sure in language strange she said,
  'I love thee true!'

'She took me to her elfin grot,
  And there she wept and sighed full sore:
And there I shut her wild, wild eyes
  With kisses four.

'And there she lullèd me asleep,
  And there I dreamed, ah woe betide!
The latest dream I ever dreamed
  On the cold hill's side.

'I saw pale kings and princes too,
  Pale warriors, death-pale were they all;
Who cried — 'La belle dame sans merci
  Hath thee in thrall!'

'I saw their starved lips in the gloam
  With horrid warning gapèd wide,
And I awoke, and found me here
  On the cold hill's side.

'And this is why I sojourn here
  Alone and palely loitering,
Though the sedge is withered from the lake,
  And no birds sing.'

To hope

When by my solitary hearth I sit,
And hateful thoughts enwrap my soul in gloom;
When no fair dreams before my mind's eye flit
And the bare heath of life presents no bloom,
Sweet Hope, ethereal balm upon me shed,
And wave thy silver pinions o'er my head.

Whene'er I wander, at the fall of night,
Where woven boughs shut out the moon's
    bright ray,
Should sad Despondency my musings fright,
And frown, to drive fair Cheerfulness away,
Peep with the moonbeams through the leafy
    roof,
And keep that fiend Despondence far aloof.

Should Disappointment, parent of Despair,
Strive for her son to seize my careless heart;
When, like a cloud, he sits upon the air,
Preparing on his spellbound prey to dart:
Chase him away, sweet Hope, with visage
    bright,
And fright him as the morning frightens night!

Whene'er the fate of those I hold most dear
Tells to my fearful breast a tale of sorrow,
O bright-eyed Hope, my morbid fancy cheer;
Let me awhile thy sweetest comforts borrow:
Thy heaven-born radiance around me shed,
And wave thy silver pinions o'er my head!

Should e'er unhappy love my bosom pain,
From cruel parents, or relentless fair;

O let me think it is not quite in vain
To sigh out sonnets to the midnight air!
Sweet Hope, ethereal balm upon me shed,
And wave thy silver pinions o'er my head!

In the long vista of the years to roll,
Let me not see our country's honour fade:
O let me see our land retain her soul,
Her pride, her freedom; and not freedom's
    shade.
From thy bright eyes unusual brightness shed
Beneath thy pinions canopy my head!

A thing of beauty *from* **Endymion**
A thing of beauty is a joy for ever:
Its loveliness increases; it will never
Pass into nothingness; but still will keep
A bower quiet for us, and a sleep
Full of sweet dreams, and health, and quiet
    breathing.
Therefore, on every morrow, are we wreathing
A flowery band to bind us to the earth,
Spite of despondence, of the inhuman dearth
Of noble natures, of the gloomy days,
Of all the unhealthy and o'er-darkened ways
Made for our searching: yes, in spite of all,
Some shape of beauty moves away the pall
From our dark spirits. Such the sun, the
    moon,
Trees old and young, sprouting a shady boon
For simple sheep; and such are daffodils
With the green world they live in; and clear
    rills
That for themselves a cooling covert make

'Gainst the hot season; the mid-forest brake,
Rich with a sprinkling of fair musk-rose
　　blooms:
And such too is the grandeur of the dooms
We have imagined for the mighty dead;
All lovely tales that we have heard or read:
An endless fountain of immortal drink,
Pouring unto us from the heaven's brink.

Nor do we merely feel the essences
For one short hour; no, even as the trees
That whisper round a temple become soon
Dear as the temple's self, so does the moon,
The passion poesy, glories infinite,
Haunt us till they become a cheering light
Unto our souls, and bound to us so fast,
That, whether there be shine, or gloom o'ercast,
They always must be with us, or we die.

Ode to a nightingale

My heart aches, and a drowsy numbness pains
My sense, as though of hemlock I had drunk,
Or emptied some dull opiate to the drains
One minute past, and Lethe-wards had sunk:
'Tis not through envy of thy happy lot,
But being too happy in thine happiness,
　　That thou, light-winged Dryad of the trees,
　　　　In some melodious plot
Of beechen green, and shadows numberless,
　　Singest of summer in full-throated ease.

O for a draught of vintage! that hath been
　　Cooled a long age in the deep-delvèd earth,
Tasting of Flora and the country green,

90

Dance, and Provençal song, and sunburnt
mirth!
O for a beaker full of the warm South!
Full of the true, the blushful Hippocrene,
With beaded bubbles winking at the brim,
And purple-stained mouth;
That I might drink, and leave the world
unseen,
And with thee fade away into the forest
dim:

Fade far away, dissolve, and quite forget
What thou among the leaves hast never
known,
The weariness, the fever and the fret
Here, where men sit and hear each other
groan;
Where palsy shakes a few, sad, last grey hairs,
Where youth grows pale, and spectre-thin, and
dies;
Where but to think is to be full of sorrow
And leaden-eyed despairs;
Where Beauty cannot keep her lustrous
eyes,
Or new love pine at them beyond tomorrow.

Away! away! for I will fly to thee,
Not charioted by Bacchus and his pards,
But on the viewless wings of Poesy,
Though the dull brain perplexes and retards:
Already with thee! tender is the night,
And haply the Queen-Moon is on her throne,
Clustered around by all her starry Fays;
But here there is no light,

Save what from heaven is with the breezes
blown
  Through verdurous glooms and winding
    mossy ways.

I cannot see what flowers are at my feet,
  Nor what soft incense hangs upon the boughs,
But, in embalmèd darkness, guess each sweet
  Wherewith the seasonable month endows
The grass, the thicket, and the fruit-tree wild;
  White hawthorn, and the pastoral eglantine;
    Fast fading violets covered up in leaves;
      And mid-May's eldest child,
    The coming musk-rose, full of dewy wine,
The murmurous haunt of flies on summer
eves.

Darkling, I listen; and for many a time
  I have been half in love with easeful death,
Called him soft names in many a musèd
rhyme,
  To take into the air my quiet breath;
Now more than ever seems it rich to die,
  To cease upon the midnight with no pain,
    While thou art pouring forth thy soul
    abroad
      In such an ecstasy!
    Still wouldst thou sing, and I have ears in
    vain —
  To thy high requiem become a sod.

Thou wast not born for death, immortal bird!
  No hungry generations tread thee down;
The voice I hear this passing night was heard

In ancient days by emperor and clown:
Perhaps the self-same song that found a path
    Through the sad heart of Ruth, when, sick for
    home,
        She stood in tears amid the alien corn;
        The same that oft-times hath
        Charmed magic casements, opening on the
        foam
Of perilous seas, in faery lands forlorn.

Forlorn! the very word is like a bell
    To toll me back from thee to my sole self!
Adieu! the fancy cannot cheat so well
    As she is famed to do, deceiving elf.
Adieu! adieu! thy plaintive anthem fades
    Past the near meadows, over the still stream,
Up the hillside; and now 'tis buried deep
    In the next valley-glades:
Was it a vision, or a waking dream?
    Fled is that music: — do I wake or sleep?

Thomas Hood (1799 – 1845)
Thomas Hood's most famous poem, *Song of the shirt*, was a great inspiration to the late eighteenth-century movement which saw the possibility of using verse as a form of social protest. It gained popularity not only in Britain but also in America and Germany, and was widely translated in Russia. Hood had been appalled by the unemployment and sexual exploitation of the time and found a unique poetic voice to express his views. Away from this serious side of his work, he was also a great lover of comic verse. That didn't always

93

endear him to his critics, but his humour and compassion won great popularity. I learnt the poem *I remember, I remember*, as a child.

I remember, I remember
I remember, I remember
The house where I was born,
The little window where the sun
Came peeping in at morn;
He never came a wink too soon,
Nor brought too long a day,
But now, I often wish the night,
Had borne my breath away!

I remember, I remember,
The roses, red and white,
The violets and the lily-cups,
Those flowers made of light!
The lilacs where the robin built,
And where my brother set
The laburnum on his birthday, —
The tree is living yet!

I remember, I remember,
Where I was used to swing,
And thought the air must rush as fresh
To swallows on the wing;
My spirit grew in feathers then,
That is so heavy now,
And summer pools could hardly cool
The fever on my brow!

I remember, I remember,
The fir trees dark and high;

94

I used to think their slender tops
Were close against the sky;
It was a childish ignorance,
But now 'tis little joy,
To know I'm farther off from heaven,
Than when I was a boy.

Silence

There is a silence where hath been no sound,
   There is a silence where no sound may be,
   In the cold grave — under the deep, deep
    sea,
Or in wide desert where no life is found,
Which hath been mute, and still must sleep
    profound;
   No voice is hushed — no life treads silently,
   But clouds and cloudy shadows wander free,
That never spoke, over the idle ground:
But in green ruins, in the desolate walls,
   Of antique palaces, where man hath been,
Though the dun fox, or wild hyena, calls,
   And owls, that flit continually between,
Shriek to the echo, and the low winds moan,
There the true silence is, self-conscious and
    alone.

Ruth

She stood breast high amid the corn,
Clasped by the golden light of morn,
Like the sweetheart of the sun,
Who many a glowing kiss had won.

On her cheek an autumn flush,
Deeply ripened — such a blush

95

In the midst of brown was born,
Like red poppies grown with corn.

Round her eyes her tresses fell,
Which were blackest none could tell,
But long lashes veiled a light,
That had else been all too bright.

And her hat, with shady brim,
Made her tressy forehead dim —
Thus she stood amid the stooks,
Praising God with sweetest looks: —

Sure, I said, heaven did not mean,
Where I reap thou shouldst but glean,
Lay thy sheaf adown and come,
Share my harvest and my home.

The song of the shirt
'With fingers weary and worn,
With eyelids heavy and red,
A woman sat, in unwomanly rags,
Plying her needle and thread.
Stitch! stitch! stitch!
In poverty, hunger, and dirt,
And still with a voice of dolorous pitch
She sang the 'Song of the shirt.'

'Work! work! work!
While the cock is crowing aloof!
And work — work — work,
Till the stars shine through the roof!
It's Oh! to be a slave
Along with the barbarous Turk,

Where woman has never a soul to save,
If this is Christian work.

'Work — work — work,
Till the brain begins to swim;
Work — work — work,
Till the eyes are heavy and dim!
Seam, and gusset, and band,
Band, and gusset, and seam,
Till over the buttons I fall asleep,
And sew them on in a dream!

'Oh, men, with sisters dear!
Oh, men, with mothers and wives!
It is not linen you're wearing out
But human creatures' lives!
Stitch — stitch — stitch,
In poverty, hunger, and dirt,
Sewing at once, with a double thread,
A shroud as well as a shirt.

'But why do I talk of death?
That phantom of grisly bone,
I hardly fear his terrible shape,
It seems so like my own
It seems so like my own,
Because of the fasts I keep;
Oh God, that bread should be so dear,
And flesh and blood so cheap!

'Work — work — work!
My labour never flags;
And what are its wages? A bed of straw,
A crust of bread — and rags.

That shattered roof — this naked floor —
A table — a broken chair —
And a wall so blank, my shadow I thank
For sometimes falling there!

'Work — work — work!
From weary chime to chime,
'Work — work — work,
As prisoners work for crime!
Band, and gusset, and seam,
Seam and gusset, and band,
Till the heart is sick, and the brain benumbed,
As well as the weary hand.

'Work — work — work!
In the dull December light,
And work — work — work,
When the weather is warm and bright
While underneath the eaves
The brooding swallows cling
As if to show me their sunny backs
And twit me with the spring.

'Oh! but to breathe the breath
Of the cowslips and primrose sweet
With the sky above my head,
And the grass beneath my feet;
For only one short hour
To feel as I used to feel,
Before I knew the woes of want
And the walk that costs a meal.

'Oh! but for one short hour!
A respite however brief!

No blessèd leisure for love or hope,
But only time for grief!
A little weeping would ease my heart,
But in their briny bed
My tears must stop, for every drop
Hinders needle and thread!

'Seam, and gusset, and band,
Band, and gusset, and seam,
Work, work, work,
Like the engine that works by steam!
A mere machine of iron and wood
That toils for mammon's sake —
Without a brain to ponder and craze
Or a heart to feel — and break!'

With fingers weary and worn,
With eyelids heavy and red,
A woman sat, in unwomanly rags,
Plying her needle and thread
Stitch! stitch! stitch!
In poverty, hunger, and dirt,
And still with a voice of dolorous pitch,
Would that its tone could reach the rich!
She sang this 'Song of the shirt!'

Anonymous (eighteenth century)
The Vicar of Bray
In good King Charles's golden days,
    When loyalty no harm meant;
A furious High-Church man I was,
    And so I gained preferment.
Unto my flock I daily preached,
    'Kings are by God appointed,

99

And damned are those who dare resist,
　Or touch the lord's anointed.'
　　And this is Law, I will maintain
　　　Unto my dying day, Sir,
　　That whatsoever King shall reign,
　I will be Vicar of Bray, Sir!

When royal James possessed the Crown,
　And Popery grew in fashion,
The Penal Law I hooted down,
　And read the Declaration:
The Church of Rome I found would fit
　Full well my constitution,
And I had been a Jesuit
But for the Revolution.
　And this is Law, etc.

When William our Deliverer came
　To heal the Nation's grievance,
I turned the cat in pan again,
　And swore to him allegiance:
Old principles I did revoke,
　Set Conscience at a distance,
Passive Obedience is a joke,
　A jest is Non-Resistance.
　　And this is Law, etc.

When glorious Anne became our Queen,
　The Church of England's glory,
Another face of things was seen,
　And I became a Tory:
Occasional Conformists base
　I damned, and Moderation,
And thought the Church in danger was

100

From such prevarication.
And this is Law, etc.

When George in pudding time came o'er,
And moderate men looked big, Sir,
My principles I changed once more,
And so became a Whig, Sir:
And thus preferment I procured
From our Faith's Great Defender,
And almost every day abjured
The Pope and the Pretender.
And this is Law, etc.

The illustrious House of Hanover,
And Protestant Succession,
To these I lustily will swear,
Whilst they can keep possession:
For in my Faith and Loyalty
I never once will falter,
But George my lawful King shall be,
Except the times should alter.
And this is Law, etc.

William Barnes (1801 – 86)
Born into a farming family, Barnes became a
remarkable scholar and founded a successful
school in Dorchester. His great interest was
language and he mastered Latin, Greek,
Italian, Welsh, Hebrew and many others. He
became obsessed with English dialect and
published much poetry in this form. He is
remembered most, however, for his poetry in
contemporary English and was an important
influence on Hardy and Tennyson.

The mother's dream (Mater dolorosa)

I'd a dream tonight
As I fell asleep,
Oh! the touching sight
Makes me still to weep:
Of my little lad,
Gone to leave me sad,
Aye, the child I had,
But was not to keep.

As in heaven high,
I my child did seek,
There, in train, came by
Children fair and meek.
Each in lily white,
With a lamp alight;
Each was clear to sight,
But they did not speak.

Then, a little sad,
Came my child in turn,
But the lamp he had,
Oh! it did not burn;
He, to clear my doubt,
Said, half turned about,
'Your tears put it out;
Mother, never mourn.'

Musings

Before the falling summer sun
   The boughs are shining all as gold,
And down below them waters run,
   As there in former years they rolled;
The poolside wall is glowing hot,

102

The pool is in a dazzling glare,
And makes it seem as ah! 'tis not,
A summer when my life was fair.

The evening, gliding slowly by,
  Seems one of those that long have fled;
The night comes on to star the sky
  As then it darkened round my head.
A girl is standing by yon door,
  As one in happy times was there,
And this day seems, but is no more,
  A day when all my life was fair.

We hear from yonder feast the hum
  Of voices, as in summers past;
And hear the beatings of the drum
  Again come throbbing on the blast.
There neighs a horse in yonder plot,
  At once there neighed our petted mare,
And summer seems, but ah! is not
  The summer when our life was fair.

The storm-wind
When the swift-rolling brook, swollen deep,
  Rushes on by the alders, full speed,
And the wild-blowing winds lowly sweep
  O'er the quivering leaf and the weed,
And the willow tree writhes in each limb
Over sedge-beds that reel by the brim —

The man that is staggering by
  Holds his hat to his head by the brim;
And the girl as her hair-locks outfly,
  Puts a foot out, to keep herself trim,

And the quivering wavelings o'erspread
The small pool where the bird dips his head.

But out at my house, in the lee
  Of the nook, where the winds die away,
The light swimming airs, round the tree
  And the low-swinging ivy stem, play
So soft that a mother that's nigh
Her still cradle, may hear her babe sigh.

Elizabeth Barrett Browning (1806 – 61)

Elizabeth was the eldest of 12 children of a famously tyrannical father, who refused to allow his progeny to marry. A sickly girl, she carried on a correspondence with Robert Browning, with whom she eventually eloped in 1846. She lived the rest of her life in Casa Guidi, in Florence, where she died in Browning's arms, 15 years later. During her life, her poetry was held in higher regard than her husband's.

A musical instrument

  What was he doing, the great god Pan,
Down in the reeds by the river?
Spreading ruin and scattering ban,
Splashing and paddling with hoofs of a goat,
And breaking the golden lilies afloat
  With the dragonfly on the river.

He tore out a reed, the great god Pan,
  From the deep cool bed of the river:
The limpid water turbidly ran,
And the broken lilies a-dying lay,

And the dragonfly had fled away,
  Ere he brought it out of the river.

High on the shore sat the the great god Pan,
  While turbidly flowed the river;
And hacked and hewed as a great god can,
With his hard bleak steel at the patient reed,
Till there was not a sign of a leaf indeed
  To prove it fresh from the river.

He cut it short, did the great god Pan
  (How tall it stood in the river!),
Then drew the pith, like the heart of a man,
Steadily from the outside ring,
And notched the poor dry empty thing
  In holes, as he sat by the river.

'This is the way,' laughed the great god Pan
  (Laughed while he sat by the river),
'The only way, since gods began
To make sweet music, they could succeed.'
Then, dropping his mouth to a hole in the
  reed,
  He blew in power by the river.

Sweet, sweet, sweet, O Pan!
  Piercing sweet by the river!
Blinding sweet, O great god Pan!
The sun on the hill forgot to die,
And the lilies revived, and the dragonfly
  Came back to dream on the river.

Yet half a beast is the great god Pan,
  To laugh as he sits by the river,

Making a poet out of a man:
The true gods sigh for the cost and pain —
For the reed which grows nevermore again
    As a reed with the reeds of the river.

Henry Wadsworth Longfellow (1807 – 82)

Henry Wadsworth Longfellow dawned on me at an early age. I remember being asked to analyse and parse the first two lines of *The village blacksmith*: 'Under a spreading chestnut-tree/ The village smithy stands.' And I was made to recite: 'The day is done, and the darkness/ Falls from the wings of Night/ As a feather is wafted downward/ From an eagle in his flight.' All this was before I became entranced by *Hiawatha*. He certainly was the 'schoolroom poet'. His greatest qualities are memorability and the irresistible music of his work. His writing is always accessible and although never regarded as great, he became the most popular nineteenth-century American poet.

The arrow and the song

I shot an arrow into the air,
It fell to earth, I knew not where;
For, so swiftly it flew, the sight
Could not follow it in its flight.

I breathed a song into the air,
It fell to earth, I knew not where;
For who has sight so keen and strong,
That it can follow the flight of song?

Long, long afterward, in an oak
I found the arrow, still unbroke;
And the song, from beginning to end,
I found again in the heart of friend.

The village blacksmith
Under a spreading chestnut tree
   The village smithy stands;
The smith, a mighty man is he,
   With large and sinewy hands;
And the muscles of his brawny arms
   Are strong as iron bands.

His hair is crisp, and black, and long,
   His face is like the tan;
His brow is wet with honest sweat,
   He earns whate'er he can,
And looks the whole world in the face,
   For he owes not any man.

Week in, week out, from morn till night,
   You can hear his bellows blow;
You can hear him swing his heavy sledge,
   With measured beat and slow,
Like a sexton ringing the village bell,
   When the evening sun is low.

And children coming home from school
   Look in at the open door;
They love to see the flaming forge,
   And hear the bellows roar,
And catch the burning sparks that fly
   Like chaff from a threshing floor.

107

He goes on Sunday to the church,
    And sits among his boys;
He hears the parson pray and preach,
    He hears his daughter's voice,
Singing in the village choir,
    And it makes his heart rejoice.

It sounds to him like her mother's voice,
    Singing in Paradise!
He needs must think of her once more,
    How in the grave she lies;
And with his hard, rough hand he wipes
    A tear out of his eyes.

Toiling — rejoicing — sorrowing,
    Onward through life he goes;
Each morning sees some task begin,
    Each evening sees it close;
Something attempted, something done,
    Has earned a night's repose.

Thanks, thanks to thee, my worthy friend,
    For the lesson thou hast taught!
Thus at the flaming forge of life
    Our fortunes must be wrought;
Thus on its sounding anvil shaped
    Each burning deed and thought.

From **The building of the ship**
Sail forth into the sea of life,
O gentle, loving, trusting wife,
And safe from all adversity
Upon the bosom of that sea
Thy comings and thy goings be!

For gentleness and love and trust
Prevail o'er angry wave and gust;
And in the wreck of noble lives
Something immortal still survives!

Thou, too, sail on, O Ship of State!
Sail on, o UNION, strong and great!
Humanity with all its fears,
With all the hopes of future years,
Is hanging breathless on thy fate!
We know what Master laid thy keel,
What Workmen wrought thy ribs of steel,
Who made each mast, and sail, and rope,
What anvils rang, what hammers beat,
In what a forge and what a heat
Were shaped the anchors of thy hope!
Fear not each sudden sound and shock,
'Tis of the wave and not the rock;
'Tis but the flapping of the sail,
And not a rent made by the gale!
In spite of rock and tempest's roar,
In spite of false lights on the shore,
Sail on, nor fear to breast the sea!
Our hearts, our hopes, are all with thee,
Our hearts, our hopes, our prayers, our tears,
Our faith triumphant o'er our fears,
Are all with thee — are all with thee!

Edgar Allan Poe (1809 – 40)
Edgar Allan Poe wanted desperately to
become one of the significant voices of
nineteenth-century poetry, but his work
attracted more criticism than praise.
T. S. Eliot was scathing: he said Poe's work

produced nothing more vivid than dreamlike impressions which seemed unconnected to life. Emerson called him 'the jingle man'. It was left to Yeats to see in Poe the flair of the great lyric poet. That kind of approbation came too late for him. Forever short of money, he died without achieving the literary prominence he sought. Perhaps the poem for which he is best known is *The raven*. It is very typical of his work.

The raven

Once upon a midnight dreary, while I pondered, weak and weary,
Over many a quaint and curious volume of forgotten lore —
While I nodded, nearly napping, suddenly there came a tapping,
As of some one gently rapping — rapping at my chamber door.
' 'Tis some visitor,' I muttered, 'tapping at my chamber door —
Only this and nothing more.'

Ah! distinctly I remember, it was in the bleak December,
And each separate dying ember wrought its ghost upon the floor.
Eagerly I wished the morrow; vainly I had sought to borrow
From my books surcease of sorrow — sorrow for the lost Lenore —
Nameless here for evermore.

And the silken, sad, uncertain rustling of each
    purple curtain
Thrilled me — filled me with fantastic terrors
    never felt before;
So that now, to still the beating of my heart, I
    stood repeating,
' 'Tis some visitor entreating entrance at my
    chamber door —
Some late visitor entreating entrance at my chamber
    door:
This it is and nothing more.'

Presently my soul grew stronger; hesitating then
    no longer,
'Sir,' said I, 'or Madam, truly your forgiveness
    I implore;
But the fact is, I was napping, and so gently
    you came rapping,
And so faintly you came tapping, tapping at my
    chamber door,
That I scarce was sure I heard you.' Here I
    opened wide the door:
Darkness there, and nothing more.

Deep into that darkness peering, long I stood
    there wondering, fearing,
Doubting, dreaming dreams no mortal ever
    dared to dream before;
But the silence was unbroken, and the darkness
    gave no token,
And the only word there spoken was the
    whispered word 'Lenore!'
This I whispered, and an echo murmured back

the word 'Lenore!'
Merely this, and nothing more.

Back into my chamber turning, all my soul
within me burning,
Soon again I heard a tapping, somewhat louder
than before.
'Surely,' said I, 'surely that is something at my
window lattice;
Let me see, then, what thereat is, and this
mystery explore —
Let my heart be still a moment, and this mystery
explore.
'Tis the wind, and nothing more.'

Open here I flung the shutter, when, with many
a flirt and flutter,
In there stepped a stately Raven of the saintly
days of yore.
Not the least obeisance made he, not an instant
stopped or stayed he;
But with mien of lord or lady, perched above
my chamber door —
Perched upon a bust of Pallas just above my
chamber door —
Perched, and sat, and nothing more.

Then this ebony bird beguiling my sad fancy
into smiling,
By the grave and stern decorum of the
countenance it wore:
'Though thy crest be shorn and shaven, thou,'
I said, 'art sure no craven;
Ghastly, grim and ancient Raven, wandering

from the nightly shore —
Tell me what thy lordly name is on the night's
Plutonian shore!'
Quoth the Raven, 'Nevermore.'

Much I marvelled this ungainly fowl to hear
discourse so plainly,
Though its answer little meaning, little relevancy
bore;
For we cannot help agreeing that no living
human being
Ever yet was blessed with seeing bird above his
chamber door —
Bird or beast upon the sculptured bust above
his chamber door,
With such name as 'Nevermore.'

But the Raven, sitting lonely on that placid bust,
spoke only
That one word, as if his soul in that one word
he did outpour.
Nothing further then he uttered, not a feather
then he fluttered —
Till I scarcely more than muttered, 'Other
friends have flown before —
On the morrow *he* will leave me, as my hopes
have flown before.'
Then the bird said, 'Nevermore.'

Startled at the stillness broken by reply so aptly
spoken,
'Doubtless,' said I, 'what it utters is its only
stock and store,
Caught from some unhappy master, whom

unmerciful disaster
Followed fast and followed faster, till his songs
one burden bore —
Till the dirges of his hope this melancholy
burden bore,
Of 'Never — nevermore'.'

But the raven still beguiling all my sad soul into
smiling,
Straight I wheeled a cushioned seat in front of
bird, and bust, and door;
Then upon the velvet sinking, I betook myself
to linking
Fancy into fancy, thinking what this ominous
bird of yore —
What this grim, ungainly, ghastly, gaunt, and
ominous bird of yore,
Meant in croaking, 'Nevermore.'

Thus I sat engaged in guessing, but no syllable
expressing
To the fowl, whose fiery eyes now burned into
my bosom's core;
This and more I sat divining, with my head at
ease reclining
On the cushion's velvet lining, that the lamplight
gloated o'er.
But whose violet velvet lining, with the lamplight
gloated o'er,
She shall press, ah, nevermore!

Then methought the air grew denser, perfumed
from an unseen censer
Swung by seraphim whose footfalls tinkled on

the tufted floor.
'Wretch,' I cried, 'thy God hath lent thee — by these angels He hath sent thee
Respite — respite and nepenthe from thy memories of Lenore!
Quaff, oh, quaff this kind nepenthe, and forget this lost Lenore!'
Quoth the Raven, 'Nevermore.'

'Prophet,' said I, 'thing of evil! — prophet still, if bird or devil! —
Whether tempter sent, or whether tempest tossed thee here ashore,
Desolate, yet all undaunted, on this desert land enchanted —
On this home by horror haunted — tell me truly, I implore —
Is there — *is* there balm in Gilead? — tell me — tell me, I implore!'
Quoth the Raven, 'Nevermore.'

'Prophet,' said I, 'thing of evil! — prophet still, if bird or devil!
By that heaven that bends above us — by that God we both adore —
Tell this soul, with sorrow laden, if, within, the distant Aidenn,
It shall clasp a sainted maiden, whom the angels name Lenore —
Clasp a rare and radiant maiden, whom the angels name Lenore?'
Quoth the Raven, 'Nevermore.'

'Be that word our sign of parting, bird of fiend,'
  I shrieked, upstarting —
'Get thee back into the tempest and the night's
  Plutonian shore!
Leave no black plume as a token of that lie thy
  soul hath spoken!
Leave my loneliness unbroken! — quit the bust
  above my door!
Take thy beak from out my heart, and take thy
  form from off my door!'
  Quoth the Raven, 'Nevermore.'

And the Raven, never flitting, still is sitting, still
  is sitting,
On the pallid bust of Pallas, just above my
  chamber door:
And his eyes have all the seeming of a demon's
  that is dreaming,
And the lamplight o'er him streaming throws
  his shadow on the floor;
And my soul from out that shadow that lies
  floating on the floor
  Shall be lifted — nevermore!

To one in paradise
Thou wast all that to me, love,
  For which my soul did pine —
A green isle in the sea, love,
  A fountain and a shrine,
All wreathed with fairy fruits and flowers,
  And all the flowers were mine.

Ah, dream too bright to last!
  Ah, starry Hope! that didst arise

116

But to be overcast!
  A voice from out the Future cries,
'On! on!' — but o'er the Past
  (Dim gulf!) my spirit hovering lies
Mute, motionless, aghast!

For, alas! alas! with me
  The light of Life is o'er!
No more — no more — no more —
(Such language holds the solemn sea
  To the sands upon the shore)
Shall bloom the thunder-blasted tree,
  Or the stricken eagle soar!

Now all my days are trances,
  And all my nightly dreams
Are where thy grey eye glances,
  And where thy footstep gleams —
In what ethereal dances,
  By what eternal streams!

A dream within a dream
Take this kiss upon the brow!
And, in parting from you now,
Thus much let me avow —
You are not wrong, who deem
That my days have been a dream:
Yet if hope has flown away
In a night, or in a day,
In a vision, or in none,
Is it therefore the less gone?
All that we see or seem
Is but a dream within a dream.

I stand amid the roar
Of a surf-tormented shore,
And I hold within my hand
Grains of the golden sand —
How few! yet how they creep
Through my fingers to the deep,
While I weep — while I weep!
O God! can I not grasp
Them with a tighter clasp?
O God! can I not save
One from the pitiless wave?
Is all that we see or seem
But a dream within a dream?

To Helen

Helen, thy beauty is to me
  Like those Nicean barks of yore,
That gently, o'er a perfumed sea,
  The weary, way-worn wanderer bore
  To his own native shore.

On desperate seas long wont to roam,
  Thy hyacinth hair, thy classic face,
Thy Naiad airs have brought me home
  To the glory that was Greece,
And the grandeur that was Rome.

Lo! in yon brilliant window niche
  How statue-like I see thee stand,
  The agate lamp within thy hand,
Ah! Psyche, from the regions which
  Are holy land!

Alfred, Lord Tennyson (1809 – 92)

It is easy to see why Tennyson was so frequently accused of silliness and intellectual provinciality. Gerard Manley Hopkins suggested that some of Tennyson's work sank 'into vulgarity' but even so ended up calling him 'a glorious poet'. Perhaps very little more needs to be said if, despite its occasional unevenness, we can still enjoy the rolling beauty of his work.

His epic poem *Idylls of the King* is a tribute to great reputation. It paints a moving picture of the end of Camelot. The king's court is overcome by deep sadness and grief, as, with lofty reflections, he prepares to take his leave. This is among the first poems I was made to learn and to recite at school. Those who taught me drew so many morals from it.

Ulysses is old and very proud of all he has done, but he is never overbearing or bombastic. There is a basic humility in all he says, and, of course, Tennyson brings the work to an end with some glorious lines about the invincibility of the human spirit.

Ulysses

It little profits that an idle king,
By this still hearth, among these barren crags,
Matched with an agèd wife, I mete and dole
Unequal laws unto a savage race,
That hoard, and sleep, and feed, and know
   not me.

I cannot rest from travel: I will drink
Life to the less: all times I have enjoyed
Greatly, have suffered greatly, both with those
That loved me, and alone; on shore, and when
Through scudding drifts and rainy Hyades
Vext the dim sea: I am become a name;
For always roaming with a hungry heart
Much have I seen and known; cities of men
And manners, climates, councils, governments,
Myself not least, but honoured of them all;
And drunk delight of battle with my peers,
Far on the ringing plains of windy Troy.

I am a part of all that I have met;
Yet all experience is an arch wherethrough
Gleams that untravelled world, whose margin
    fades
For ever and for ever when I move.
How dull it is to pause, to make an end,
To rust unburnished, not to shine in use!
As though to breathe were life. Life piled
    on life
Were all too little, and of one to me
Little remains: but every hour is saved
From that eternal silence, something more,
A bringer of new things; and vile it were
For some three suns to store and hoard myself,
And this grey spirit yearning in desire
To follow knowledge like a sinking star,
Beyond the utmost bound of human thought.

This is my son, my own Telemachus,
To whom I leave the sceptre and the isle —
Well-loved of me, discerning to fulfil

This labour, by slow prudence to make mild
A rugged people, and through soft degrees
Subdue them to the useful and the good.
Most blameless is he, centred in the sphere
Of common duties, decent not to fail
In offices of tenderness, and pay
Meet adoration to my household gods,
When I am gone. He works his work, I mine.

There lies the port; the vessel puffs her sail:
There gloom the dark broad seas. My mariners,
Souls that have toiled, and wrought, and thought
    with me —
That ever with a frolic welcome took
The thunder and the sunshine, and opposed
Free hearts, free foreheads — you and I are
    old;
Old age hath yet his honour and his toil;
Death closes all: but something ere the end,
Some work of noble note, may yet be done,
Not unbecoming men that strove with Gods.

The lights begin to twinkle from the rocks:
The long day wanes: the slow moon climbs:
    the deep
Moans round with many voices. Come, my
    friends,
'Tis not too late to seek a newer world.
Push off, and sitting well in order smite
The sounding furrows; for my purpose holds
To sail beyond the sunset, and the baths
Of all the western stars, until I die.
It may be that the gulfs will wash us down:
It may be we shall touch the Happy Isles,

And see the great Achilles, whom we knew.
Though much is taken, much abides; and
  though
We are not now that strength which in old
  days
Moved earth and heaven; that which we are,
  we are;
One equal temper of heroic hearts,
Made weak by time and fate, but strong in
  will
To strive, to seek, to find, and not to yield.

From **The passing of Arthur**
And slowly answered Arthur from the barge:
'The old order changeth, yielding place to
  new,
And God fulfils Himself in many ways,
Lest one good custom should corrupt the world.
Comfort thyself: what comfort is in me?
I have lived my life, and that which I have
  done
May He within Himself make pure! but thou —
If thou shouldst never see my face again,
Pray for my soul. More things are wrought by
  prayer
Than this world dreams of. Wherefore, let thy
  voice
Rise like a fountain for me night and day.
For what are men better than sheep or goats
That nourish a blind life within the brain,
If, knowing God, they lift not hands of prayer
Both for themselves and those who call them
  friend?
For so the whole round earth is every way

Bound by gold chains about the feet of God.
But now farewell. I am going a long way
With those thou seest — if indeed I go —
(For all my mind is clouded with a doubt)
To the island-valley of Avilion;
Where falls not hail, or rain, or any snow,
Nor ever wind blows loudly, but it lies
Deep-meadow'd, happy, fair with orchard-lawns
And bowery hollows crowned with summer
    sea,
Where I will heal me of my grievous wound.'
So said he, and the barge with oar and sail
Moved from the brink, like some full-breasted
    swan
That, fluting a wild carol ere her death,
Ruffles her pure cold plume, and takes the
    flood
With swarthy webs. Long stood Sir Bedivere
Revolving many memories, till the hull
Looked one black dot against the verge of
    dawn,
And on the mere the wailing died away.

Here ended Hall, and our last light, that long
Had wink'd and threaten'd darkness, flared and
    fell:
At which the Parson, sent to sleep with sound,
And waked with silence, grunted 'Good!' but we
Sat rapt: it was the tone with which he read —
Perhaps some modern touches here and there
Redeem'd it from the charge of nothingness —
Or else we loved the man and prized his work;
I know not: but we sitting, as I said,
The cock crew loud; as at that time of year

The lusty bird takes every hour for dawn:
Then Francis, muttering, like a man ill-used,
'There now — that's nothing!' drew a little
  back,
And drove his heel into the smoulder'd log
That sent a blast of sparkles up the flue
And so to bed; where yet in sleep I seem'd
To sail with Arthur under looming shores,
Point after point; till on to dawn, when dreams
Begin to feel the truth and stir of day,
To me, methought, who waited with a crowd,
There came a bark that, blowing forward, bore
King Arthur, like a modern gentleman
Of stateliest port; and all the people cried
'Arthur is come again: he cannot die.'
Then those that stood upon the hills behind
Repeated — 'Come again and thrice as fair;'
And, further inland, voices echoed — 'Come
With all good things, and war shall be no more.'
At this a hundred bells began to peal,
That with the sound I woke, and heard indeed
The clear church-bells ring in the Christmas morn.

Crossing the bar
Sunset and evening star,
  And one clear call for me!
And may there be no moaning of the bar,
  When I put out to sea,

But such a tide as moving seems asleep,
  Too full for sound and foam,
When that which drew from out the boundless
  deep
    Turns again home.

Twilight and evening bell,
　　And after that the dark!
And may there be no sadness of farewell,
　　When I embark;

For though from out our bourne of time and
　　place
　　The flood may bear me far,
I hope to see my Pilot face to face
　　When I have crossed the bar.

The lady of Shalott

PART I

On either side the river lie
Long fields of barley and of rye,
That clothe the wold and meet the sky;
And through the field the road runs by
　　To many-towered Camelot;
And up and down the people go,
Gazing where the lilies blow
Round an island there below,
　　The island of Shalott.

Willows whiten, aspens quiver,
Little breezes dusk and shiver
Through the wave that runs for ever
By the island in the river
　　Flowing down to Camelot.
Four grey walls, and four grey towers,
Overlook a space of flowers,
And the silent isle imbowers
　　The Lady of Shalott.

By the margin, willow-veiled,
Slide the heavy barges trailed
By slow horses; and unhailed
The shallop flitteth silken-sailed
    Skimming down to Camelot:
But who hath seen her wave her hand?
Or at the casement seen her stand?
Or is she known in all the land,
    The Lady of Shalott?

Only reapers, reaping early
In among the bearded barley,
Hear a song that echoes cheerly
From the river winding clearly,
    Down to towered Camelot:
And by the moon the reaper weary,
Piling sheaves in uplands airy,
Listening, whispers ' 'Tis the fairy
    Lady of Shalott.'

PART II
There she weaves by night and day
A magic web with colours gay.
She has heard a whisper say,
A curse is on her if she stay
    To look down to Camelot.
She knows not what the curse may be,
And so she weaveth steadily,
And little other care hath she,
    The Lady of Shalott.

And moving through a mirror clear
That hangs before her all the year,
Shadows of the world appear.

There she sees the highway near
   Winding down to Camelot:
There the river eddy whirls,
And there the surly village-churls,
And the red cloaks of market girls,
   Pass onward from Shalott.

Sometimes a troop of damsels glad,
An abbot on an ambling pad,
Sometimes a curly shepherd-lad,
Or long-haired page in crimson clad,
   Goes by to towered Camelot;
And sometimes through the mirror blue
The knights come riding two and two:
She hath no loyal knight and true,
   The Lady of Shalott.

But in her web she still delights
To weave the mirror's magic sights,
For often through the silent nights
A funeral, with plumes and lights
   And music, went to Camelot:
Or when the moon was overhead,
Came two young lovers lately wed;
'I am half sick of shadows,' said
   The Lady of Shalott.

PART III

A bow-shot from her bower-eaves,
He rode between the barley-sheaves,
The sun came dazzling through the leaves,
And flamed upon the brazen greaves
   Of bold Sir Lancelot.
A red-cross knight for ever kneeled

To a lady in his shield,
That sparkled on the yellow field,
  Beside remote Shalott.

The gemmy bridle glittered free,
Like to some branch of stars we see
Hung in the golden galaxy.
The bridle bells rang merrily
  As he rode down to Camelot:
And from his blazoned baldric slung
A mighty silver bugle hung,
And as he rode his armour rung,
  Beside remote Shalott.

All in the blue unclouded weather
Thick-jewelled shone the saddle-leather,
The helmet and the helmet-feather
Burned like one burning flame together,
  As he rode down to Camelot.
As often through the purple night,
Below the starry clusters bright,
Some bearded meteor, trailing light,
  Moves over still Shalott.

His broad clear brow in sunlight glowed;
On burnished hooves his war-horse trod;
From underneath his helmet flowed
His coal-black curls as on he rode,
  As he rode down to Camelot.
From the bank and from the river
He flashed into the crystal mirror,
'Tirra lirra,' by the river
  Sang Sir Lancelot.

She left the web, she left the loom,
She made three paces through the room,
She saw the water-lily bloom,
She saw the helmet and the plume,
  She looked down to Camelot.
Out flew the web and floated wide;
The mirror cracked from side to side;
'The curse is come upon me!' cried
  The Lady of Shalott.

PART IV

In the stormy east-wind straining,
The pale yellow woods were waning,
The broad stream in his banks complaining,
Heavily the low sky raining
  Over towered Camelot;
Down she came and found a boat
Beneath a willow left afloat,
And round about the prow she wrote
  The Lady of Shalott.

And down the river's dim expanse —
Like some bold seer in a trance,
Seeing all his own mischance —
With a glassy countenance
  Did she look to Camelot.
And at the closing of the day
She loosed the chain, and down she lay;
The broad stream bore her far away,
  The Lady of Shalott.

Lying, robed in snowy white
That loosely flew to left and right —
The leaves upon her falling light —

Through the noises of the night
  She floated down to Camelot:
And as the boat-head wound along
The willowy hills and fields among,
They heard her singing her last song,
  The Lady of Shalott.

Heard a carol, mournful, holy,
Chanted loudly, chanted lowly,
Till her blood was frozen slowly,
And her eyes were darkened wholly,
  Turned to towered Camelot.
For ere she reached upon the tide
The first house by the waterside,
Singing in her song she died,
  The Lady of Shalott.

Under tower and balcony,
By garden-wall and gallery,
A gleaming shape she floated by,
Dead-pale between the houses high,
  Silent into Camelot.
Out upon the wharfs they came,
Knight and burgher, lord and dame,
And round the prow they read her name,
  The Lady of Shalott.

Who is this? and what is here?
And in the lighted palace near
Died the sound of royal cheer;
And they crossed themselves for fear,
  All the knights at Camelot:
But Lancelot mused a little space;
He said, 'She has a lovely face;

God in his mercy lend her grace,
  The Lady of Shalott.'

Robert Browning (1812 – 89)

Robert Browning's work has always been
associated in my mind with his dramatic
elopement, at the age of 33, with Elizabeth
Barrett.

It must have been an extraordinarily bold
thing to do in the middle of the nineteenth
century. It contributed partly to his reputation
as a truly 'romantic' poet, with an abiding
passion for people and the complexities of
human nature. He seemed to know instinctively
why people acted as they did. Poetry came to
him naturally: he wrote copiously, almost
impetuously, and with penetrating insight,
even from his deathbed.

My star

All that I know
  Of a certain star,
Is, it can throw
  (Like the angled spar)
Now a dart of red,
  Now a dart of blue,
Till my friends have said
  They would fain see, too.
My star that dartles the red and the blue!
Then it stops like a bird; like a flower, hangs
  furled;
  They must solace themselves with the Saturn
  above it.
What matter to me if their star is a world?

Mine has opened its soul to me; therefore I
love it.

Meeting at night

I

The grey sea and the long black land;
And the yellow half-moon large and low;
And the startled little waves that leap
In fiery ringlets from their sleep,
As I gain the cove with pushing prow,
And quench its speed in the slushy sand.

II

Then a mile of warm sea-scented beach;
Three fields to cross till a farm appears;
A tap at the pane, the quick sharp scratch
And blue spurt of a lighted match,
And a voice less loud, through its joys and
  fears,
Than the two hearts beating each to each!

In three days

I

So, I shall see her in three days
And just one night, but nights are short,
Then two long hours, and that is morn.
See how I come, unchanged, unworn!
Feel, where my life broke off from thine,
How fresh the splinters keep and fine —
Only a touch, and we combine!

II

Too long, this time of year, the days!
But nights, at least the nights are short.

132

As night shows where her one moon is,
A hand's-breadth of pure light and bliss,
So life's night gives my lady birth
And my eyes hold her! What is worth
The rest of heaven, the rest of earth?

III
O loaded curls, release your store
Of warmth and scent, as once before
The tingling hair did, lights and darks
Outbreaking into fairy sparks,
When under curl and curl I pried
After the warmth and scent inside,
Through lights and darks how manifold —
The dark inspired, the light controlled!
As early Art embrowned the gold.

IV
What great fear, should one say, 'Three days
That change the world might change as well
Your fortune; and if joy delays,
Be happy that no worse befell!'
What small fear, if another says,
'Three days and one short night beside
May throw no shadow on your ways;
But years must teem with change untried,
With chance not easily defied,
With an end somewhere undescried.'
No fear! — or if a fear be born
This minute, it dies out in scorn.
Fear? I shall see her in three days
And one night, now the nights are short,
Then just two hours, and that is morn.

133

The lost leader

I

Just for a handful of silver he left us,
    Just for a riband to stick in his coat —
Found the one gift of which fortune bereft us,
    Lost all the others she lets us devote;
They, with the gold to give, doled him out silver,
    So much was theirs who so little allowed:
How all our copper had gone for his service!
    Rags — were they purple, his heart had been proud!
We that had loved him so, followed him, honoured him,
    Lived in his mild and magnificent eye,
Learned his great language, caught his clear accents,
    Made him our pattern to live and to die!
Shakespeare was of us, Milton was for us,
    Burns, Shelley, were with us — they watch from their graves!
He alone breaks from the van and the freemen —
    He alone sinks to the rear and the slaves!

II

We shall march prospering — not through his presence;
    Songs may inspirit us — not from his lyre;
Deeds will be done — while he boasts his quiescence,
    Still bidding crouch whom the rest bade aspire:
Blot out his name, then, record one lost soul more,

One task more declined, one more footpath
untrod,
One more devils' triumph and sorrow for angels,
    One wrong more to man, one more insult
to God!
Life's night begins: let him never come back
to us!
    There would be doubt, hesitation and pain,
Forced praise on our part — the glimmer of
twilight,
    Never glad confident morning again!
Best fight on well, for we taught him — strike
gallantly,
    Menace our heart ere we master his own;
Then let him receive the new knowledge and
wait us,
    Pardoned in heaven, the first by the throne!

Edward Lear (1812 – 88)

Born in London, Lear was a world-traveller,
writer and wonderful artist. He suffered from
epilepsy and depression, and perhaps his much-
loved nonsense verse was an escape from this
unpleasant reality. I can only concur with the
sentiment: 'How pleasant to know Mr Lear.'

How pleasant to know Mr Lear

How pleasant to know Mr Lear!
    Who has written such volumes of stuff!
Some think him ill-tempered and queer,
    But a few think him pleasant enough.

His mind is concrete and fastidious,
    His nose is remarkably big;

His visage is more or less hideous,
    His beard it resembles a wig.

He has ears, and two eyes, and ten fingers,
    Leastways if you reckon two thumbs;
Long ago he was one of the singers,
    But now he is one of the dumbs.

He sits in a beautiful parlour,
    With hundreds of books on the wall;
He drinks a great deal of Marsala,
    But never gets tipsy at all.

He has many friends, laymen and clerical,
    Old Foss is the name of his cat:
His body is perfectly spherical,
    He weareth a runcible hat.

When he walks in a waterproof white,
    The children run after him so!
Calling out, 'He's come out in his night-
    Gown, that crazy old Englishman, oh!'

He weeps by the side of the ocean,
    He weeps on the top of his hill;
He purchases pancakes and lotion,
    And chocolate shrimps from the mill.

He reads but he cannot speak Spanish,
    He cannot abide ginger-beer:
Ere the days of his pilgrimage vanish,
    How pleasant to know Mr Lear!

Emily Brontë (1818 – 48)
In a life lasting only 30 years, Emily Brontë managed to produce, in *Wuthering Heights*, one of the best-loved novels in English and some of the most original poetry of the nineteenth century. She was closest to her sister Anne (their invented land of Gondal is the scene of some of Emily's finest poetry), but it was Charlotte who encouraged the publication of her poems. Emily never knew success in her lifetime and I wonder what she would make of the worldwide fame her work now enjoys.

Remembrance
Cold in the earth — and the deep snow piled
    above thee,
Far, far removed, cold in the dreary grave!
Have I forgot, my only love, to love thee,
Severed at last by time's all-severing wave?

Now, when alone, do my thoughts no longer
    hover
Over the mountains, on that northern shore,
Resting their wings where heath and fern-leaves
    cover
Thy noble heart for ever, ever more?

Cold in the earth — and fifteen wild Decembers
From those brown hills have melted into
    spring —
Faithful indeed is the spirit that remembers
After such years of change and suffering!

Sweet love of youth, forgive if I forget thee
While the world's tide is bearing me along:
Other desires and other hopes beset me,
Hopes which obscure, but cannot do thee wrong!

No later light has lightened up my heaven;
No second morn has ever shone for me:
All my life's bliss from thy dear life was
    given —
All my life's bliss is in the grave with thee.

But, when the days of golden dreams had
    perished,
And even despair was powerless to destroy,
Then did I learn how existence could be
    cherished,
Strengthened and fed without the aid of joy;

Then did I check the tears of useless passion,
Weaned my young soul from yearning after
    thine;
Sternly denied its burning wish to hasten
Down to that tomb already more than mine!

And, even yet, I dare not let it languish,
Dare not indulge in memory's rapturous pain;
Once drinking deep of that divinest anguish,
How could I seek the empty world again?

Spellbound
The night is darkening round me,
The wild winds coldly blow;
But a tyrant spell has bound me
And I cannot, cannot go.

138

The giant trees are bending
Their bare boughs weighed with snow.
And the storm is fast descending,
And yet I cannot go.

Clouds beyond clouds above me,
Wastes beyond wastes below;
But nothing drear can move me;
I will not, cannot go.

Last lines
'The following are the last lines my sister Emily
ever wrote.' (*Charlotte Brontë*)

No coward soul is mine,
No trembler in the world's storm-troubled
    sphere:
I see Heaven's glories shine,
And Faith shines equal, arming me from Fear.

O God within my breast,
Almighty, ever-present Deity!
Life — that in me has rest,
As I — Undying Life — have power in Thee!

Vain are the thousand creeds
That move men's hearts: unutterably vain;
Worthless as withered weeds,
Or idlest froth amid the boundless main,

To waken doubt in one
Holding so fast by thine infinity;
So surely anchored on
The steadfast rock of Immortality.

With wide-embracing love
Thy spirit animates eternal years,
Pervades and broods above,
Changes, sustains, dissolves, creates and rears.

Though earth and man were gone,
And suns and universes ceased to be,
And Thou were left alone,
Every Existence would exist in Thee.

There is not room for Death,
Nor atom that his might could render void:
Thou — Thou art Being and Breath,
And what Thou art may never be destroyed.

Walt Whitman (1819 – 92)

Whitman's experience as a poet was shaped
in the hard school of the American Civil War.
He saw its brutality, and as a poet he was
determined that 'these dead shall not have
died in vain'. But the war also defined his
firm and guiding concepts of sovereignty,
democracy and liberty. He came to believe
that nations could not be half free or half
democratic and felt, like John Stuart Mill, that
human nature must have its full play 'to
expand in numberless and even conflicting
directions'. He was very fond of Lincoln and
very depressed by his death.

The joy of his work is its sense of style,
grace and wonder and the touching faith that
made him the poet of democracy.

When lilacs last in the dooryard bloom'd
(*From* Memories of President Lincoln)

When lilacs last in the dooryard bloomed,
And the great star early drooped in the western
    sky in the night,
I mourned, and yet shall mourn with ever-
    returning spring.

Ever-returning spring, trinity sure to me you bring,
Lilac blooming prennial and drooping star in
    the west,
And thought of him I love.

O Captain! My Captain!

O Captain! my Captain! our fearful trip is done,
The ship has weathered every rack, the prize we
    sought is won,
The port is near, the bells I hear, the people all
    exulting,
While follow eyes the steady keel, the vessel grim
    and daring;
    But O heart! heart! heart!
    O the bleeding drops of red,
    Where on the deck my Captain lies,
    Fallen cold and dead.

O Captain! my Captain! rise up and hear the
    bells;
Rise up — for you the flag is flung — for you
    the bugle trills,
For you bouquets and ribboned wreaths — for
    you the shores a-crowding,
For you they call, the swaying mass, their eager
    faces turning;

141

Here Captain! dear father!
This arm beneath your head!
It is some dream that on the deck,
You've fallen cold and dead.

My Captain does not answer, his lips are pale
   and still,
My father does not feel my arm, he has no pulse
   nor will;
The ship is anchor'd safe and sound, its voyage
   closed and done,
From fearful trip the victor ship comes in with
   object won;
   Exult O shores, and sing, O bells!
   But I, with mournful tread,
   Walk the deck my Captain lies,
   Fallen cold and dead.

George Eliot (Mary Ann Evans) (1819 – 80)

George Eliot was one of the finest writers
produced by Victorian England. Her novels
were both critically and commercially
successful and, though her poetry is less well
known, it too is of the highest quality.

   She was a radical free-thinker for her time
and scandalised her family by living with a
man who was not her husband. Readers
familiar with her novels will recognise the
same themes cropping up in her poetry.

Brother and sister

I
I cannot choose but think upon the time
When our two lives grew like two buds that kiss

142

At lightest thrill from the bee's swinging chime,
Because the one so near the other is.

He was the elder and a little man
Of forty inches, bound to show no dread,
And I the girl that puppy-like now ran,
Now lagged behind my brother's larger tread.

I held him wise, and when he talked to me
Of snakes and birds, and which God loved
     the best,
I thought his knowledge marked the boundary
Where men grew blind, though angels knew
     the rest.

If he said 'Hush!' I tried to hold my breath;
Wherever he said 'Come!' I stepped in faith.

II
Long years have left their writing on my brow,
But yet the freshness and the dew-fed beam
Of those young mornings are about me now,
When we two wandered toward the far-off
     stream

With rod and line. Our basket held a store
Baked for us only, and I thought with joy
That I should have my share, though he had
     more,
Because he was the elder and a boy.

The firmaments of daisies since to me
Have had those mornings in their opening
     eyes,

The bunchèd cowslip's pale transparency
Carries that sunshine of sweet memories,

And wild-rose branches take their finest scent
From those blest hours of infantine content.

III
Our mother bade us keep the trodden ways,
Stroked down my tippet, set my brother's frill,
Then with the benediction of her gaze
Clung to us lessening, and pursued us still

Across the homestead to the rookery elms,
Whose tall old trunks had each a grassy mound,
So rich for us, we counted them as realms
With varied products: here were earth-nuts
  found,

And here the ladyfingers in deep shade;
Here sloping toward the moat the rushes grew,
The large to split for pith, the small to braid;
While over all the dark rooks cawing flew,

And made a happy strange solemnity,
A deep-toned chant from life unknown to me.

IV
Our meadow-path had memorable spots:
One where it bridged a tiny rivulet,
Deep hid by tangled blue forget-me-nots;
And all along the waving grasses met

My little palm, or nodded to my cheek,
When flowers with upturned faces gazing drew

My wonder downward, seeming all to speak
With eyes of souls that dumbly heard and
knew.

Then came the copse, where wild things rushed
unseen,
And black-scathed grass betrayed the past abode
Of mystic gypsies, who still lurked between
Me and each hidden distance of the road.

A gypsy once had startled me at play,
Blotting with her dark smile my sunny day.

v
Thus rambling we were schooled in deepest
lore,
And learned the meanings that give words a
soul,
The fear, the love, the primal passionate store,
Whose shaping impulses make manhood whole.

Those hours were seed to all my after good;
My infant gladness, through eye, ear, and touch,
Took easily as warmth a various food
To nourish the sweet skill of loving much.

For who in age shall roam the earth and find
Reasons for loving that will strike out love
With sudden rod from the hard year-pressed
mind?
Were reasons sown as thick as stars above,

'Tis love must see them, as the eye sees light:
Day is but number to the darkened sight.

VI

Our brown canal was endless to my thought;
And on its banks I sat in dreamy peace,
Unknowing how the good I loved was wrought,
Untroubled by the fear that it would cease.

Slowly the barges floated into view
Rounding a grassy hill to me sublime
With some unknown beyond it, whither flew
The parting cuckoo toward a fresh springtime.

The wide-arched bridge, the scented elderflowers,
The wondrous watery rings that died too soon,
The echoes of the quarry, the still hours
With white robe sweeping on the shadeless
    noon,

Were but my growing self, are part of me,
My present past, my root of piety.

VII

Those long days measured by my little feet
Had chronicles which yield me many a text;
Where irony still finds an image meet
Of full-grown judgements in this world perplexed.

One day my brother left me in high charge,
To mind the rod, while he went seeking bait,
And bade me, when I saw a nearing barge,
Snatch out the line, lest he should come too
    late.

Proud of the task, I watched with all my
    might

146

For one whole minute, till my eyes grew wide,
Till sky and earth took on a strange new light
And seemed a dream-world floating on some
   tide —

A fair pavilioned boat for me alone
Bearing me onward through the vast unknown.

VIII
But sudden came the barge's pitch-black prow,
Nearer and angrier came my brother's cry,
And all my soul was quivering fear, when lo!
Upon the imperilled line, suspended high,

A silver perch! My guilt that won the prey,
Now turned to merit, had a guerdon rich
Of songs and praises, and made merry play,
Until my triumph reached its highest pitch

When all at home were told the wondrous
   feat,
And how the little sister had fished well.
In secret, though my fortune tasted sweet,
I wondered why this happiness befell.

'The little lass had luck,' the gardener said:
And so I learned, luck was with glory wed.

IX
We had the selfsame world enlarged for each
By loving difference of girl and boy:
The fruit that hung on high beyond my reach
He plucked for me, and oft he must employ

A measuring glance to guide my tiny shoe
Where lay firm stepping-stones, or call to mind
'This thing I like my sister may not do,
For she is little, and I must be kind.'

Thus boyish will the nobler mastery learned
Where inward vision over impulse reigns,
Widening its life with separate life discerned,
A like unlike, a self that self restrains.

His years with others must the sweeter be
For those brief days he spent in loving me.

x

His sorrow was my sorrow, and his joy
Sent little leaps and laughs through all my
    frame;
My doll seemed lifeless and no girlish toy
Had any reason when my brother came.

I knelt with him at marbles, marked his fling
Cut the ringed stem and make the apple drop,
Or watched him winding close the spiral string
That looped the orbits of the humming top.

Grasped by such fellowship my vagrant thought
Ceased with dream-fruit dream-wishes to fulfil;
My aery-picturing fantasy was taught
Subjection to the harder, truer skill

That seeks with deeds to grave a thought-tracked
    line,
And by 'What is,' 'What will be' to define.

XI

School parted us; we never found again
That childish world where our two spirits
  mingled
Like scents from varying roses that remain
One sweetness, nor can evermore be singled.

Yet the twin habit of that early time
Lingered for long about the heart and tongue:
We had been natives of one happy clime
And its dear accent to our utterance clung.

Till the dire years whose awful name is Change
Had grasped our souls still yearning in divorce,
And pitiless shaped them in two forms that
  range
Two elements which sever their life's course.

But were another childhood-world my share,
I would be born a little sister there.

Matthew Arnold (1822 – 88)
Arnold was the son of the great reforming
educator, Thomas Arnold, who had a lasting
influence on education in Britain. After a
great academic career, he was an inspector of
schools for 35 years, travelling the length and
breadth of the country and gaining the
experience of 'real life', which informs his
poetry. Much of *Dover Beach* was written on
his honeymoon.

Requiescat
Strew on her roses, roses,

149

And never a spray of yew.
In quiet, she reposes:
  Ah! would that I did too.

Her mirth the world required;
  She bathed it in smiles of glee.
But her heart was tired, tired,
  And now they let her be.

Her life was turning, turning,
  In mazes of heat and sound.
But for peace her soul was yearning,
  And now peace laps her round.

Her cabined, ample spirit,
  It fluttered and failed for breath.
Tonight it doth inherit
  The vasty hall of death.

Dover Beach

The sea is calm tonight.
The tide is full, the moon lies fair
Upon the Straits — on the French coast the
  light
Gleams and is gone; the cliffs of England
  stand,
Glimmering and vast, out in the tranquil bay.
Come to the window, sweet is the night air!
Only, from the long line of spray
Where the sea meets the moon-blanched land,
Listen! you hear the grating roar
Of pebbles which the waves draw back, and
  fling,
At their return, up the high strand,

Begin and and cease, and then again begin,
With tremulous cadence slow, and bring
The eternal note of sadness in.

Sophocles long ago
Heard it on the Aegean and it brought
Into his mind the turbid ebb and flow
Of human misery; we
Find also in the sound a thought,
Hearing it by this distant northern sea.

The sea of faith
Was once, too, at the full, and round earth's
    shore
Lay like the folds of a bright girdle furled.
But now I only hear
Its melancholy, long, withdrawing roar,
Retreating, to the breath
Of the night-wind, down the vast edges drear
And naked shingles of the world.

Ah, love, let us be true
To one another! for the world, which seems
To lie before us like a land of dreams,
So various, so beautiful, so new,
Hath really neither joy, nor love, nor light,
Nor certitude, nor peace, nor help for pain;
And we are here as on a darkling plain
Swept with confused alarms of struggle and
    flight,
Where ignorant armies clash by night.

The last word
Creep into thy narrow bed,

Creep, and let no more be said!
Vain thy onset! all stands fast.
Thou thyself must break at last.

Let the long contention cease!
Geese are swans, and swans are geese.
Let them have it how they will!
Thou art tired; best be still.

They outtalked thee, hissed thee, tore thee?
Better men fared thus before thee;
Fired their ringing shot and passed,
Hotly charged — and sank at last.

Charge once more, then, and be dumb!
Let the victors, when they come,
When the forts of folly fall,
Find thy body by the wall!

William Allingham (1824 – 89)
An Irishman, Allingham settled in England in
1863. The first four lines of *The fairies* are
some of the most remembered in light poetry.

The fairies
Up the airy mountain,
    Down the rushy glen,
We daren't go a-hunting
    For fear of little men;
Wee folk, good folk,
    Trooping all together;
Green jacket, red cap,
    And white owl's feather!

Down along the rocky shore
  Some make their home,
They live on crispy pancakes
  Of yellow tide-foam;
Some in the reeds
  Of the black mountain lake,
With frogs for their watchdogs,
  All night awake.

High on the hilltop
  The old King sits;
He is now so old and grey
  He's nigh lost his wits.
With a bridge of white mist
  Columbkill he crosses,
On his stately journeys
  From Slieveleague to Rosses;
Or going up with music
  On cold starry nights
To sup with the Queen
  Of the gay Northern Lights.

They stole little Bridget
  For seven years long;
When she came down again
  Her friends were all gone.
They took her lightly back,
  Between the night and morrow,
They thought that she was fast asleep,
  But she was dead with sorrow.
They have kept her ever since
  Deep within the lake,
On a bed of flag-leaves,
  Watching till she wake.

By the craggy hillside,
  Through the mosses bare,
They have planted thorn trees
  For pleasure here and there.
Is any man so daring
  As dig them up in spite,
He shall find their sharpest thorns
  In his bed at night.

Up the airy mountain,
  Down the rushy glen,
We daren't go a-hunting
  For fear of little men;
Wee folk, good folk,
  Trooping all together;
Green jacket, red cap,
  And white owl's feather!

Dante Gabriel Rossetti (1828 – 82)

Although born in England, Rossetti was the
son of an Italian patriot and his romantic life
betrayed his Latin blood. He began his
creative life as a painter and formed the Pre-
Raphaelite Brotherhood with, amongst others,
Holman Hunt and John Everett Millais. His
first poetry was published in 1850, the year he
met his future wife, Elizabeth Siddall.

A great beauty, she was the model for the
drowned Ophelia in the famous Millais
painting. When she died in 1862 an
inconsolable Rossetti buried a manuscript
containing many poems with her. Rather
unchivalrously, but to the joy of all poetry
lovers, he exhumed the poems some seven years

154

later and published them the following year.

In his day, Rossetti's work was attacked as obscene and scandalous, ridiculous charges but the power and eroticism of his work is still striking.

An old song ended
'*How should I your true love know*
    From another one?
'*By his cockle-bat and staff*
    And his sandal-shoon.'

'And what signs have told you now
    That he hastens home?'
'Lo! the spring is nearly gone,
    He is nearly come.'

'For a token is there nought,
    Say, that he should bring?'
'He will bear a ring I gave
    And another ring.'

'How may I, when he shall ask,
    Tell him who lies there?'
'Nay, but leave my face unveiled
    And unbound my hair.'

'Can you say to me some word
    I shall say to him?'
'Say I'm looking in his eyes
    Though my eyes are dim.'

Even so
    So it is, my dear.

All such things touch secret strings
For heavy hearts to hear.
So it is, my dear.

    Very like indeed:
Sea and sky, afar, on high,
    Sand and strewn seaweed —
    Very like indeed.

    But the sea stands spread
As one wall with the flat skies,
Where the lean black craft like flies
    Seem well-nigh stagnated,
    Soon to drop off dead.

    Seemed it so to us
When I was thine and thou wast mine,
    And all these things were thus,
    But all our world in us?

    Could we be so now?
Not if all beneath heaven's pall
    Lay dead but I and thou,
    Could we be so now!

Sudden light
I have been here before,
    But when or how I cannot tell:
I know the grass beyond the door,
    The sweet keen smell,
The sighing sound, the lights around the shore.

You have been mine before —
    How long ago I may not know:

156

But just when at that swallow's soar
  Your neck turned so,
Some veil did fall — I knew it all of yore.

Has this been thus before?
  And shall not thus time's eddying flight
Still with our lives our love restore
  In death's despite,
And day and night yield one delight once
  more?

Christina Rossetti (1830 – 94)
Like her brother, Christina was brought up in
a rarefied, intellectual atmosphere. She was
never a healthy woman and her life lacked
fulfilment. This affected her verse which is
melancholy and touchingly sad.

Uphill
Does the road wind uphill all the way?
  Yes, to the very end.
Will the day's journey take the whole long day?
  From morn to night, my friend.

But is there for the night a resting-place?
  A roof for when the slow, dark hours begin.
May not the darkness hide it from my face?
  You cannot miss that inn.

Shall I meet other wayfarers at night?
  Those who have gone before.
Then must I knock, or call when just in sight?
  They will not keep you standing at that
  door.

Shall I find comfort, travel-sore and weak?
 Of labour you shall find the sum.
Will there be beds for me and all who seek?
 Yea, beds for all who come.

Somewhere or other
Somewhere or other there must surely be
 The face not seen, the voice not heard,
The heart that not yet — never yet — ah me!
 Made answer to my word.

Somewhere or other, may be near or far;
 Past land and sea, clean out of sight;
Beyond the wandering moon, beyond the star
 That tracks her night by night.

Somewhere or other, may be far or near;
 With just a wall, a hedge, between;
With just the last leaves of the dying year
 Fallen on a turf grown green.

Emily Dickinson (1830 – 86)
A lawyer's daughter, this American poet was a
lively and cheerful youth who suddenly
withdrew from the world in her twenties,
eventually avoiding all contact and never
leaving home. Her life is, consequently,
something of a mystery: why did she lock
herself up? Was it a tragic romance? We shall
never know. Only a handful of her poems
were published in her lifetime, but after her
death some 2,000 poems, neatly arranged in
packets, were found.
 Her inner life was clearly one of raging

emotions which she expresses with the greatest originality in her work.

The coming of the night
How the old mountains drip with sunset
And the break of dun!
How the hemlocks are tipped in tinsel
By the wizard sun!

How the old steeples hand the scarlet,
Till the ball is full,
Have I the lip of the flamingo
That I dare to tell?

Then, how the fire ebbs like billows,
Touching all the grass
With a departing, sapphire feature,
As if a duchess pass!

How a small dusk crawls on the village
Till the houses blot;
And the odd flambeaux no men carry
Glimmer on the spot!

Now it is night in nest and kennel,
And where was the wood,
Just a dome of abyss is nodding
Into solitude!

These are the visions baffled Guido;
Titian never told;
Domenichino dropped the pencil,
Powerless to unfold.

There came a wind like a bugle
from **The storm**
There came a wind like a bugle;
It quivered through the grass,
And a green chill upon the heat
So ominous did pass
We barred the windows and the doors
As from an emerald ghost,
The doom's electric moccasin
That very instant passed.
On a strange mob of panting trees,
And fences fled away,
And rivers where the houses ran
The living looked that day.
The bell within the steeple wild
The flying tidings whirled,
How much can come
And much can go,
And yet abide the world!

There's a certain slant of light
There's a certain slant of light,
On winter afternoons,
That oppresses, like the weight
Of cathedral tunes.

Heavenly hurt it gives us;
We can find no scar,
But internal difference,
Where the meanings are.

None may teach it anything,
'Tis the seal, despair,

An imperial affliction
Sent us of the air.

When it comes, the landscape listens,
Shadows hold their breath;
When it goes, 'tis like the distance
On the look of death.

Lewis Carroll (1832 – 98)
Carroll was the pen-name of C. L. Dodgson,
a lecturer in mathematics at Oxford. The
classic tale, *Alice's Adventures in Wonderland*,
was published in 1865. Dodgson was a
pioneering photographer, whose interest in
young girls is much speculated upon.

The White Knight's song
I'll tell thee everything I can:
    There's little to relate,
I saw an agèd agèd man,
    A-sitting on a gate.
'Who are you, agèd man?' I said.
    'And how is it you live?'
And his answer trickled through my head,
    Like water through a sieve.

He said 'I look for butterflies
    That sleep among the wheat:
I make them into mutton-pies,
    And sell them in the street.
I sell them unto men', he said,
    'Who sail on stormy seas;
And that's the way I get my bread —
    A trifle, if you please.'

But I was thinking of a plan
  To dye one's whiskers green,
And always use so large a fan
  That they could not be seen.
So, having no reply to give
  To what the old man said,
I cried 'Come, tell me how you live!'
  And thumped him on the head.

His accents mild took up the tale:
  He said 'I go my ways,
And when I find a mountain-rill,
  I set it in a blaze;
And thence they make a stuff they call
  Rowland's Macassar-Oil —
Yet two-pence-halfpenny is all
  They give me for my toil.'

But I was thinking of a way
  To feed oneself on batter
And so go on from day to day
  Getting a little fatter.
I shook him well from side to side,
  Until his face was blue:
'Come, tell me how you live,' I cried,
  'And what it is you do!'

He said 'I hunt for haddocks' eyes
  Among the heather bright,
And work them into waistcoat-buttons
  In the silent night.
And these I do not sell for gold
  Or coin of silvery shine,

But for a copper halfpenny,
    And that will purchase nine.

'I sometimes dig for buttered rolls,
    Or set limed twigs for crabs:
I sometimes search the grassy knolls
    For wheels of hansom cabs.
And that's the way' (he gave a wink)
    'By which I get my wealth —
And very gladly will I drink
    Your Honour's noble health.'

I heard him then, for I had just
    Completed my design
To keep the Menai bridge from rust
    By boiling it in wine.
I thanked him much for telling me
    The way he got his wealth,
But chiefly for his wish that he
    Might drink my noble health.

And now, if e'er by chance I put
    My fingers into glue,
Or madly squeeze a right-hand foot
    Into a left-hand shoe,
Or if I drop upon my toe
    A very heavy weight,
I weep, for it reminds me so
Of that old man I used to know —
Whose look was mild, whose speech was slow
Whose hair was whiter than the snow,
Whose face was very like a crow,
With eyes, like cinders, all aglow,
Who seemed distracted with his woe,

Who rocked his body to and fro,
And muttered mumblingly and low,
As if his mouth were full of dough,
Who snorted like a buffalo —
That summer evening long ago,
    A-sitting on a gate.

A.C. Swinburne (1837 – 1909)

Algernon Charles Swinburne was a genius and
not too concerned about demonstrating the
fact. He had an extraordinary memory and
would recite his own poems or Greek verse
for long periods. Only his appearance let him
down. 'Not quite human', wrote one
authority, and another described him as 'a
kind of apparition in the world of mortals'.
But his poems created a dazzling excitement,
both in structure and content, so much so
that critics wondered whether the world might
not at some stage become sated with such
brilliance. It never did, and Swinburne
continued throughout his life to make
confident pronouncements on art and life and
to reign supreme.

A leave-taking

Let us go hence, my songs; she will not hear.
Let us go hence together without fear;
Keep silence now, for singing-time is over,
And over all old things and all things dear.
She loves not you nor me as we all love her.
Yea, though we sang as angels in her ear,
    She would not hear.

Let us rise up and part; she will not know.
Let us go seaward as the great winds go,
Full of blown sand and foam; what help is
    here?
There is no help, for all these things are so,
And all the world is bitter as a tear.
And how these things are, though ye strove to
    show,
    She would not know.

Let us go home and hence; she will not weep.
We gave love many dreams and days to keep,
Flowers without scent, and fruits that would
    not grow,
Saying, 'If thou wilt, thrust in thy sickle and
    reap.'
All is reaped now; no grass is left to mow;
And we that sowed, though all we fell on
    sleep,
    She would not weep.

Let us go hence and rest; she will not love.
She shall not hear us if we sing hereof,
Nor see love's ways, how sore they are and
    steep.
Come hence, let be, lie still; it is enough.
Love is a barren sea, bitter and deep;
And though she saw all heaven in flower
    above,
    She would not love.

Let us give up, go down; she will not care.
Though all the stars made gold of all the air,
And the sea moving saw before it move

One moon-flower making all the foam-flowers
    fair;
Though all those waves went over us, and
    drove
Deep down the stifling lips and drowning hair,
    She would not care.

Let us go hence, go hence; she will not see.
Sing all once more together; surely she,
She too, remembering days and words that
    were,
Will turn a little towards us, sighing; but we,
We are hence, we are gone, as though we had
    not been there.
Nay, and though all men seeing had pity on
    me,
    She would not see.

Love and sleep
Lying asleep between the strokes of night
I saw my love lean over my sad bed,
Pale as the duskiest lily's leaf or head,
Smooth-skinned and dark, with bare throat
    made to bite,
Too wan for blushing and too warm for white,
But perfect coloured without white or red.
And her lips opened amorously, and said —
I wist not what, saving one word — Delight.

And all her face was honey to my mouth,
And all her body pasture to mine eyes;
The long lithe arms and hotter hands than
    fire,
The quivering flanks, hair smelling of the south,

The bright light feet, the splendid supple thighs
And glittering eyelids of my soul's desire.

From **The garden of Proserpine**
Here, where the world is quiet;
   Here, where all trouble seems
Dead winds' and spent waves' riot
   In doubtful dreams of dreams;
I watch the green field growing
For reaping folk and sowing,
For harvest-time and mowing,
   A sleepy world of streams.

I am tired of tears and laughter,
   And men that laugh and weep;
Of what may come hereafter
   For men that sow to reap:
I am weary of days and hours,
Blown buds of barren flowers,
Desires and dreams and powers
   And everything but sleep.

Here life has death for neighbour,
   And far from eye or ear
Wan waves and wet winds labour,
   Weak ships and spirits steer;
They drive adrift and whither
They wot not who make thither;
But no such winds blow hither,
   And no such things grow here.

No growth of moor or coppice,
   No heather-flower or vine,
But bloomless buds of poppies,

Green grapes of Proserpine,
Pale beds of blowing rushes
Where no leaf blooms or blushes
Save this whereout she crushes
    For dead men deadly wine.

Pale without name or number,
    In fruitless fields of corn,
They bow themselves and slumber
    All night till light is born;
And like a soul belated,
In hell and heaven unmated,
By cloud and mist abated
    Comes out of darkness morn.

Thomas Hardy (1840 – 1928)

Son of a Dorset stonemason, Hardy worked as an architect before the success of *Far from the Madding Crowd* enabled him to write full-time.

His first volume of verse, *Wessex Poems*, was published in 1898. In his day, Hardy's verse was considered of little interest compared to his prose. Nevertheless he eventually published over 900 poems of the highest quality. Hardy disdained the 'elevated' style of his contemporaries and tried to write verse which was closer to speech patterns.

The house of hospitalities

Here we broached the Christmas barrel,
Pushed up the charred log-ends;
Here we sang the Christmas carol,
And called in friends.

Time has tired me since we met here
When the folk now dead were young,
Since the viands were outset here
And quaint songs sung.

And the worm has bored the viol
That used to lead the tune,
Rust eaten out the dial
That struck night's noon.

Now no Christmas brings in neighbours,
And the New Year comes unlit;
Where we sang the mole now labours,
And spiders knit.

Yet at midnight if here walking,
When the moon sheets wall and tree,
I see forms of old time talking,
Who smile on me.

In Tenebris I
Wintertime nighs;
  But my bereavement-pain
It cannot bring again:
  Twice no one dies.

  Flower-petals flee;
But, since it once hath been,
No more that severing scene
  Can harrow me.

  Birds faint in dread:
I shall not lose old strength

169

In the lone frost's black length:
   Strength long since fled!

Leaves freeze to dun;
But friends can not turn cold
This season as of old
   For him with none.

Tempests may scath;
But love can not make smart
Again this year his heart
   Who no heart hath.

Black is night's cope;
But death will not appal
One who, past doubtings all,
   Waits in unhope.

Great things

Sweet cyder is a great thing,
   A great thing to me,
Spinning down to Weymouth town
   By Ridgway thirstily,
And maid and mistress summoning
   Who tend the hostelry:
O cyder is a great thing,
   A great thing to me!

The dance it is a great thing,
   A great thing to me,
With candles and partners fit
   For night-long revelry;
And going home when day-dawning
   Peels pale upon the lea:

O dancing is a great thing,
  A great thing to me!

Love is, yea, a great thing,
  A great thing to me,
When, having drawn across the lawn
  In darkness silently,
A figure flits like one a-wing
  Out from the nearest tree:
O love is, yes, a great thing,
  A great thing to me!

Will these be always great things,
  Great things to me? . . .
Let it befall that One will call,
  'Soul, I have need of thee':
What then? Joy-jaunts, impassioned flings
  Love, and its ecstasy,
Will always have been great things,
  Great things to me!

In time of 'The breaking of nations'
Only a man harrowing clods
  In a slow and silent walk
With an old horse that stumbles and nods
  Half asleep as they stalk.

Only thin smoke without flame
  From the heaps of couch-grass;
Yet this will go onward the same
  Though Dynasties pass.

Yonder a maid and her wight
  Come whispering by:

War's annals will cloud into night
  Ere their story die.

Alice Meynell (1847 – 1922)

Although she came from a very privileged
background, Alice Meynell was amongst the
hardest-working writers of her time. A devout
Roman Catholic, she devoted much time and
effort to various Catholic journals. She and
her husband, Wilfrid Meynell, founded the
literary magazine *Merry England* in 1883.
Between giving birth to seven children she
also produced several volumes of poetry which
were very well received. She was nominated
twice, in 1895 and 1913, for the post of Poet
Laureate.

Renouncement

I must not think of thee; and, tired yet strong,
I shun the thought that lurks in all delight —
The thought of thee — and in the blue Heaven's
  height,
And in the sweetest passage of a song.
O just beyond the fairest thoughts that throng
This breast, the thought of thee waits hidden
  yet bright;
But it must never, never come in sight;
I must stop short of thee the whole day long.
But when sleep comes to close each difficult
  day,
When night gives pause to the long watch
  I keep
And all my bonds I needs must loose apart,
Must doff my will as raiment laid away —

172

With the first dream that comes with the first
   sleep
I run, I run, I am gathered to thy heart.

Robert Louis Stevenson (1850 – 94)
Stevenson's enduring popularity is due to his
prose works, beginning with *Treasure Island*
and including *Dr Jekyll and Mr Hyde*. His
poetry is worth a look though, for its warm
Scottish sentiment and memorable lines such as:
'Home is the sailor, home from sea,
And the hunter home from the hill.'

Requiem
Under the wide and starry sky,
   Dig the grave and let me lie:
Glad did I live and gladly die,
   And I laid me down with a will.

This be the verse you grave for me:
Here he lies where he longed to be;
Home is the sailor, home from sea,
   And the hunter home from the hill.

From **Sing me a song**
Sing me a song of a lad that is gone,
   Say, could that lad be I?
Merry of soul he sailed on a day
   Over the sea to Skye.

Mull was astern, Rhum on the port,
   Eigg on the starboard bow;
Glory of youth glowed in his soul:
   Where is that glory now?

Sing me a song of a lad that is gone,
  Say, could that lad be I?
Merry of soul he sailed on a day
  Over the sea to Skye.

Oscar Wilde (1854 – 1900)
Oscar Wilde's career was cut short by such
sensational scandal that for a time his
brilliance was obscured by the nature of his
demise. But brilliant he was without question.
He dazzled nineteenth-century society with his
devotion to aestheticism — 'art for art's sake'
— and his biting wit. On arriving in New
York in 1882 he is thought to have said, 'I
have nothing to declare but my genius.' That
ability to shock, clever though it was, did not
always win him friends. But his comedy *The
Importance of Being Earnest*, his novel *The
Picture of Dorian Gray*, and his moving *De
Produndis*, written in prison, are all classics.
So is *The ballad of Reading Gaol*, extracted
here, but which should be enjoyed in its
entirety.

From **The ballad of Reading Gaol**
And he of the swollen purple throat,
  And the stark and staring eyes,
Waits for the holy hands that took
  The Thief to Paradise;
And a broken and a contrite heart
  The Lord will not despise.

The man in red who reads the Law
  Gave him three weeks of life,

174

Three little weeks in which to heal
  His soul of his soul's strife,
And cleanse from every blot of blood
  The hand that held the knife.

And with tears of blood he cleansed the hand,
  The hand that held the steel:
For only blood can wipe out blood,
  And only tears can heal:
And the crimson stain that was of Cain
  Became Christ's snow-white seal.

In Reading gaol by Reading town
  There is a pit of shame,
And in it lies a wretched man
  Eaten by teeth of flame,
In a burning winding-sheet he lies,
  And his grave has got no name.

And there, till Christ call forth the dead,
  In silence let him lie:
No need to waste the foolish tear,
  Or heave the windy sigh:
The man had killed the thing he loved,
  And so he had to die.

And all men kill the thing they love,
  By all let this be heard,
Some do it with a bitter look,
  Some with a flattering word,
The coward does it with a kiss,
  The brave man with a sword!

A. E. Housman (1859 – 1936)

Above all else A. E. Housman believed that poetry should be accessible to all people and not just the preserve of the literary world. Housman, the ultimate literary craftsman, devoted his life to poetry after the emotional trauma of failing to win the affection of the one he loved. He immersed himself in the study of Latin, became a celebrated teacher of the language and used its discipline to inform and to shape his poetry. His work was distinguished by its precision. Yet it lost none of its grace, its charm or its delicate beauty. He wrote about the countryside and used its manifest glories as the background for his human subjects. But thoughts of divinity were never far from his mind. He went from being a great admirer of the Church of England, which he described as 'much the best religion I have ever come across' to being a confirmed sceptic.

Housman was a complex character whose work was given somewhat mixed reviews. One called him 'an absolute schizophrenic', though the balance was redressed by another who saw in what he wrote 'the making of pure verse and pure scholarship' — an undoubted credit to any great talent.

Bredon Hill

In summertime on Bredon
   The bells they sound so clear;
Round both the shires they ring them
   In steeples far and near,
   A happy noise to hear.

Here of a Sunday morning
   My love and I would lie,
And see the coloured counties,
   And hear the larks so high
   About us in the sky.

The bells would ring to call her
   In valleys miles away:
'Come all to church, good people;
   Good people, come and pray.'
   But here my love would stay.

And I would turn and answer
   Among the springing thyme,
'Oh, peal upon our wedding,
   And we will hear the chime,
   And come to church in time.'

But when the snows at Christmas
   On Bredon top were strewn,
My love rose up so early
   And stole out unbeknown
   And went to church alone.

They tolled the one bell only,
   Groom there was none to see,
The mourners followed after,
   And so to church went she,
   And would not wait for me.

The bells they sound on Bredon,
   And still the steeples hum.
'Come all to church, good people' —

Oh, noisy bells, be dumb;
I hear you, I will come.

Last poems, XXXIV — The first of May
The orchards half the way
  From home to Ludlow fair
Flowered on the first of May
  In Mays when I was there;
And seen from stile or turning
  The plume of smoke would show
Where fires were burning
  That went out long ago.

The plum broke forth in green,
  The pear stood high and snowed,
My friends and I between
  Would take the Ludlow road;
Dressed to the nines and drinking
  And light in heart and limb,
And each chap was thinking
  The fair was held for him.

Between the trees in flower
  New friends at fairtime tread
The way where Ludlow tower
  Stands planted on the dead.
Our thoughts, a long while after,
  They think, our words they say;
Theirs now's the laughter,
  The fair, the first of May.

Ay, yonder lads are yet
  The fools that we were then;
For oh, the sons we get

Are still the sons of men.
The sumless tale of sorrow
    Is all unrolled in vain:
May comes tomorrow
    And Ludlow fair again.

Untitled verse
Tell me not here, it needs not saying,
    What tune the enchantress plays
In aftermaths of soft September
    Or under blanching mays,
For she and I were long acquainted
    And I knew all her ways.

On russet floors, by waters idle,
    The pine lets fall its cone;
The cuckoo shouts all day at nothing
    In leafy dells alone;
And traveller's joy beguiles in autumn
    Hearts that have lost their own.

On acres of the seeded grasses
    The changing burnish heaves;
Or marshalled under moons of harvest
    Stand still all night the sheaves;
Or beeches strip in storms for winter
    And stain the wind with leaves.

Possess, as I possessed a season,
    The countries I resign,
Where over elmy plains the highway
    Would mount the hills and shine,
And full of shade the pillared forest
    Would murmur and be mine.

For nature, heartless, witless nature,
  Will neither care nor know
What stranger's feet may find the meadow
  And trespass there and go,
Nor ask amid the dews of morning
  If they are mine or no.

Easter hymn

If in that Syrian garden, ages slain,
You sleep, and know not you are dead in
  vain,
Nor even in dreams behold how dark and
  bright
Ascends in smoke and fire by day and night
The hate you died to quench and could but
  fan,
Sleep well and see no morning, son of man.

But if, the grave rent and the stone rolled by,
At the right hand of majesty on high
You sit, and sitting so remember yet
Your tears, your agony and bloody sweat,
Your cross and passion and the life you gave,
Bow hither out of heaven and see and save.

A. B. 'Banjo' Paterson (1864 – 1941)

Australians insist, with good reason, that the
poems of Banjo Paterson are the equal in
English literature of the work of Rudyard
Kipling. 'Banjo' was the pseudonym under
which Paterson first came to public attention
in *The Bulletin* in 1889. The rest, as they
say, is history.

  Using in full measure the tradition of the

Australian Bush ballads, Paterson became the national poet of Australia. He wrote *Waltzing Matilda* and also *The man from Snowy River* and became the authentic voice of the vast and forbidding Australian outback. His poetry is to be enjoyed for its bravado and style.

A mountain station

I bought a run a while ago
    On country rough and ridgy,
Where wallaroos and wombats grow —
    The Upper Murrumbidgee.
The grass is rather scant, it's true,
    But this a fair exchange is,
The sheep can see a lovely view
    By climbing up the ranges.

And She-oak Flat's the station's name,
    I'm not surprised at that, sirs:
The oaks were there before I came,
    And I supplied the flat, sirs.
A man would wonder how it's done,
    The stock so soon decreases —
They sometimes tumble off the run
    And break themselves to pieces.

I've tried to make expenses meet,
    But wasted all my labours;
The sheep the dingoes didn't eat
    Were stolen by the neighbours.
They stole my pears — my native pears —
    Those thrice convicted felons,
And ravished from me unawares
    My crop of paddy-melons.

181

And sometimes under sunny skies,
  Without an explanation,
The Murrumbidgee used to rise
  And overflow the station.
But this was caused (as now I know)
  When summer sunshine glowing
Had melted all Kiandra's snow
  And set the river going.

Then in the news, perhaps, you read:
  'Stock Passing. Puckawidgee,
Fat cattle: Seven hundred head
  Swept down the Murrumbidgee;
Their destination's quite obscure,
  But, somehow, there's a notion.
Unless the river falls, they're sure
  To reach the Southern Ocean.'

So after that I'll give it best;
  No more with fate I'll battle.
I'll let the river take the rest,
  For those were all my cattle.
And with one comprehensive curse
  I close my brief narration,
And advertise it in my verse —
  'For Sale! A Mountain Station.'

W. B. Yeats (1865 – 1939)

Yeats set the standard and the reputation by
which all Irish poets were judged. He was
indisputably the colossus. His work was so all
encompassing that it almost had the effect of
exhausting the genre.

  The freshness and youthful idealism of his

poem *To Ireland in the coming times* stands in sharp contrast to the bitterness of *Easter 1916* and his lines that a 'terrible beauty is born'.

The people of Ireland have always regarded William Butler Yeats as one of the finest poets of all time. Their view was supported by none other than T. S. Eliot. He described Yeats as the greatest poet writing in the English language and went on to suggest that as far as he was able to judge, he was the greatest poet 'in any language'. That is high praise indeed, and it is marvellous to discover that Yeats more than justifies it. He was brilliantly creative, and felt so deeply about poetry that he believed it was capable of transcending all the problems of Irish national life.

To Ireland in the coming times
Know, that I would accounted be
True brother of a company
That sang, to sweeten Ireland's wrong,
Ballad and story, rann and song;
Nor be I any less of them,
Because the red-rose-bordered hem
Of her, whose history began
Before God made the angelic clan,
Trails all about the written page.
When Time began to rant and rage
The measure of her flying feet
Made Ireland's heart begin to beat;
And Time bade all his candles flare
To light a measure here and there;

And may the thoughts of Ireland brood
Upon a measured quietude.

Nor may I less be counted one
With Davis, Mangan, Ferguson,
Because, to him who ponders well,
My ryhmes more than their rhyming tell
Of things discovered in the deep,
Where only body's laid asleep.
For the elemental creatures go
About my table to and fro,
That hurry from unmeasured mind
To rant and rage in flood and wind;
Yet he who treads in measured ways
May surely barter gaze for gaze.
Man ever journeys on with them
After the red-rose bordered hem.
Ah, faeries, dancing under the moon,
A Druid land, a Druid tune!

While still I may, I write for you
The love I lived, the dream I knew,
From our birthday, until we die,
Is but the winking of an eye;
And we, our singing and our love,
What measurer Time has lit above,
And all benighted things that go
About my table to and fro
Are passing on to where may be,
In truth's consuming ecstasy,
No place for love and dream at all;
For God goes by with white footfall.
I cast my heart into my rhymes,
That you, in the dim coming times,

May know how my heart went with them
After the red-rose-bordered hem.

Easter 1916

I have met them at close of day
Coming with vivid faces
From counter or desk among grey
Eighteenth-century houses.
I have passed with a nod of the head
Or polite meaningless words,
Or have lingered a while and said
Polite meaningless words,
And thought before I had done
Of a mocking tale or a gibe
To please a companion
Around the fire at the club,
Being certain that they and I
But lived where motley is worn:
All changed, changed utterly:
A terrible beauty is born.

That woman's days were spent
In ignorant goodwill,
Her nights in argument
Until her voice grew shrill.
What voice more sweet than hers
When, young and beautiful,
She rode to harriers?
This man had kept a school
And rode our wingèd horse;
This other his helper and friend
Was coming into his force;
He might have won fame in the end,
So sensitive his nature seemd,

So daring and sweet his thought.
This other man I had dreamed
A drunken, vainglorious lout.
He had done most bitter wrong
To some who are near my heart,
Yet I number him in the song;
He, too, has resigned his part
In the casual comedy;
He, too, has been changed in his turn,
Transformed utterly:
A terrible beauty is born.

Hearts with one purpose alone
Through summer and winter seem
Enchanted to a stone
To trouble the living stream.
The horse that comes from the road,
The rider, the birds that range
From cloud to tumbling cloud,
Minute by minute they change;
A shadow of cloud on the stream
Changes minute by minute;
A horse-hoof slides on the brim,
And a horse plashes within it;
The long-legged moorhens dive,
And hens to moorcocks call;
Minute by minute they live:
The stone's in the midst of all.

Too long a sacrifice
Can make a stone of the heart.
O when may it suffice?
That is Heaven's part, our part
To murmur name upon name,

As a mother names her child
When sleep at last has come
On limbs that had run wild.
What is it but nightfall?
No, no, not night but death;
Was it needless death after all?
For England may keep faith
For all that is done and said.
We know their dream; enough
To know they dreamed and are dead;
And what if excess of love
Bewildered them till they died?
I write it out in a verse —
MacDonagh and MacBride
And Connolly and Pearse
Now and in time to be,
Wherever green is worn,
Are changed, changed utterly:
A terrible beauty is born.

When you are old
When you are old and grey and full of sleep,
And nodding by the fire, take down this book,
And slowly read, and dream of the soft look
Your eyes had once, and of their shadows
   deep;

How many loved your moments of glad grace,
And loved your beauty, with love false or true,
But one man loved the pilgrim soul in you,
And loved the sorrows of your changing face;

And bending down beside the glowing bars,
Murmur, a little sadly, how Love fled

And paced upon the mountains overhead
And hid his face amid a crowd of stars.

Rudyard Kipling (1865 – 1936)
Eliot argued that Kipling frequently wrote
'verse' that was not 'poetry'. This, he went on
to suggest, did not represent failure as a poet,
because Kipling was much more concerned
about what he had to say than about whether
it was said in what might be called a pure,
poetic form.

However we choose to characterise his views
today, he was a writer of integrity. His
observations about this world and the great
events of his time are never shallow or
ephemeral. They were acute and often biting.
And so much of what he wrote is beautifully
memorable.

It is probably quite outside the school of
modern politically correct learning to recognise
and to praise poetry of an admonitory nature.
Although of this genre, for me, Kipling's *If*
has hardly ever been surpassed. It was one of
those poems I was made to memorise and to
recite. My parents probably felt if I did that,
I might absorb all that Kipling intended about
the way we should conduct our lives. I am
sure I never did, but I've always been
conscious of the simplicity and beauty of its
sentiments. It was not untypical of Kipling's
work and a few of his critics didn't take too
kindly to its tone. But its popularity over the
years is evidence enough of its durability.

If

If you can keep your head when all about you
Are losing theirs and blaming it on you,
If you can trust yourself when all men doubt
   you,
But make allowance for their doubting too;
If you can wait and not be tired by waiting,
Or being lied about, don't deal in lies,
Or being hated, don't give way to hating,
And yet don't look too good, nor talk too
   wise:

If you can dream — and not make dreams your
   master;
If you can think — and not make thoughts
   your aim;
If you can meet with Triumph and Disaster
And treat those two impostors just the same;
If you can bear to hear the truth you've
   spoken
Twisted by knaves to make a trap for fools,
Or watch the things you gave your life to,
   broken,
And stoop and build 'em up with worn-out
   tools:

If you can make one heap of all your winnings
And risk it on one turn of pitch-and-toss,
And lose, and start again at your beginnings
And never breathe a word about your loss;
If you can force your heart and nerve and
   sinew
To serve your turn long after they are gone,
And so hold on when there is nothing in you

Except the Will which says to them: 'Hold
  on!'

If you can talk with crowds and keep your
  virtue,
Or walk with Kings — nor lose the common
  touch,
If neither foes nor loving friends can hurt you,
If all men count with you, but none too much;
If you can fill the unforgiving minute
With sixty seconds' worth of distance run,
Yours is the Earth and everything that's in it,
And — which is more — you'll be a Man,
  my son!

Gethsemane (1914 – 18)
The garden called Gethsemane
In Picardy it was,
And there the people came to see
The English soldiers pass.

We used to pass — we used to pass
Or halt, as it might be,
And ship our masks in case of gas
Beyond Gethsemane.

The Garden called Gethsemane,
It held a pretty lass,
But all the time she talked to me
I prayed my cup might pass.
The officer sat on the chair,
The men lay on the grass,
And all the time we halted there
I prayed my cup might pass.

It didn't pass — it didn't pass —
It didn't pass from me.
I drank it when we met the gas
Beyond Gethsemane.

From **Epitaphs of the War 1914 – 18**

'EQUALITY OF SACRIFICE'
A. 'I was a Have.' B. 'I was a 'Have-not'.'
(*Together*) 'What hast thou given which I gave
  not?'

THE COWARD
I could not look on Death, which being known,
Men led me to him, blindfold and alone.

THE BEGINNER
On the first hour of my first day
In the front trench I fell.
(Children in boxes at a play
Stand up to watch it well.)

THE REFINED MAN
I was of delicate mind. I stepped aside for my
needs,
Disdaining the common office. I was seen from
afar and killed . . .
How is this matter for mirth? Let each man be
judged by his deeds.
I have paid my price to live with myself on the
terms that I willed.

COMMON FORM
If any question why we died,
Tell them because our fathers lied.

The Fabulists

When all the world would keep a matter hid,
Since Truth is seldom friend to any crowd,
Men write in fable, as old Æsop did,
Jesting at that which none will name aloud.
And this they needs must do, or it will fall
Unless they please they are not heard at all.

When desperate Folly daily laboureth
To work confusion upon all we have,
When diligent Sloth demandeth Freedom's death,
And banded Fear commandeth Honour's grave —
Even in that certain hour before the fall,
Unless men please they are not heard at all.

Needs must all please, yet some not all for
    need,
Needs must all toil, yet some not all for gain,
But that men taking pleasure may take heed,
Whom present toil shall snatch from later pain.
Thus some have toiled, but their reward was
    small
Since, though they pleased, they were not heard
    at all.

This was the lock that lay upon our lips,
This was the yoke that we have undergone,
Denying us all pleasant fellowships
As in our time and generation
Our pleasures unpursued age past recall,
And for our pains we are not heard at all.

What man hears aught except the groaning
    guns?

What man heeds aught save what each instant
    brings?
When each man's life all imaged life outruns,
What man shall pleasure in imaginings?
So it hath fallen, as it was bound to fall,
We are not, nor we were not, heard at all.

Hilaire Belloc (1870 – 1953)

Belloc, who was for a time a Liberal MP,
could turn his hand to virtually any form of
writing, including novels, biography, travel and
religion. It is his poetry, though, which has
passed the test of time, especially *Tarantella*,
which is included here.

Tarantella

Do you remember an Inn,
Miranda?
Do you remember an Inn?
And the tedding and the spreading
Of the straw for a bedding,
And the fleas that tease in the High Pyrenees,
And the wine that tasted of the tar?
And the cheers and the jeers of the young
    muleteers
(Under the vine of the dark verandah)?
Do you remember an Inn, Miranda
Do you remember an Inn?
And the cheers and the jeers of the young
    muleteers
Who hadn't got a penny,
And who weren't paying any,
And the hammer at the doors and the Din?
And the Hip! Hop! Hap!

Of the clap
Of the hands to the twirl and the swirl
Of the girl gone chancing,
Glancing,
Dancing,
Backing and advancing,
Snapping of a clapper to the spin
Out and in —
And the Ting, Tong, Tang of the Guitar
Do you remember an Inn,
Miranda?
Do you remember an Inn?

Never more;
Miranda,
Never more.
Only the high peaks hoar:
And Aragon a torrent at the door.
No sound
In the walls of the Halls where falls
The tread
Of the feet of the dead to the ground
No sound:
But the boom
Of the far Waterfall like Doom.

The garden party
The rich arrived in pairs
And also in Rolls-Royces;
They talked of their affairs
In loud and strident voices.

(The Husbands and the Wives
Of this select society

Lead independent lives
Of infinite variety.)

The Poor arrived in Fords,
Whose features they resembled;
They laughed to see so many Lords
And Ladies all assembled.

The People in Between
Looked underdone and harassed.
And out of place and mean,
And horribly embarrassed.

For the hoary social curse
Gets hoarier and hoarier,
And it stinks a trifle worse
Than in the days of Queen Victoria,
When they married and gave in marriage,
They danced at the County Ball,
And some of them kept a carriage.
And the flood destroyed
them all.

Walter De la Mare (1873 – 1956)
A Kentish lad, De la Mare went from school
into the oil industry; a job he kept until he
found success as a poet in his late thirties. De
la Mare was almost unique in his ability to
reach both adults and children successfully; his
poems are as likely to be found in collections
of nursery rhymes as in anthologies of adult
poetry.
   The two poems I have chosen would appeal
to adults and young people in equal measure.

195

John Mouldy

I spied John Mouldy in his cellar
Deep down twenty steps of stone;
In the dusk he sat a-smiling,
Smiling there alone.

He read no book, he snuffed no candle;
The rats ran in, the rats ran out;
And far and near, the drip of water
Went whisp'ring about.

The dusk was still, with dew a-falling,
I saw the Dog-star bleak and grim,
I saw a slim brown rat of Norway
Creep over him.

I spied John Mouldy in his cellar,
Deep down twenty steps of stone;
In the dusk he sat a-smiling,
Smiling there alone.

All that's past

Very old are the woods;
    And the buds that break
Out of the briar's boughs,
    When March winds wake,
So old with their beauty are —
    Oh, no man knows
Through what wild centuries
    Roves back the rose.

Very old are the brooks;
    And the rills that rise
Where snow sleeps cold beneath

The azure skies
Sing such a history
    Of come and gone,
Their every drop is as wise
    As Solomon.

Very old are we men
    Our dreams are tales
Told in dim Eden
    By Eve's nightingales;
We wake and whisper awhile,
    But, the day gone by,
Silence and sleep like fields
    Of amaranth lie.

Robert Frost (1874 – 1963)
By all accounts Robert Frost was a difficult
character. His life in rural New England made
him self-sufficient, a little tetchy and happy in
his own company. His long walks on his own
fired his poetic drive. He was deeply attached
to nature and to natural things and had a
genius for describing them. 'The woods are
lovely, dark and deep,/ But I have promises to
keep,/ And miles to go before I sleep.'
    His early work in America found no critical
audience. But in England before the First
World War — he lived in Buckinghamshire
for a while — he found a publisher and well-
deserved prominence.

The road not taken
Two roads diverged in a yellow wood,
And sorry I could not travel both

And be one traveller, long I stood
And looked down one as far as I could
To where it bent in the undergrowth;

Then took the other, as just as fair,
And having perhaps the better claim,
Because it was grassy and wanted wear;
Though as for that, the passing there
Had worn them really about the same,

And both that morning equally lay
In leaves no step had trodden black.
Oh, I kept the first for another day!
Yet knowing how way leads on to way,
I doubted if I should ever come back.

I shall be telling this with a sigh
Somewhere ages and ages hence:
Two roads diverged in a wood, and I —
I took the one less travelled by,
And that has made all the difference.

Gathering leaves
Spades take up leaves
No better than spoons,
And bags full of leaves
Are light as balloons.

I make a great noise
Of rustling all day
Like rabbit and deer
Running away.

But the mountains I raise
Elude my embrace,
Flowing over my arms
And into my face,

I may load and unload
Again and again
Till I fill the whole shed,
And what have I then?

Next to nothing for weight,
And since they grew duller
From contact with earth,
Next to nothing for colour.

Next to nothing for use.
But a crop is a crop,
And who's to say where
The harvest shall stop?

Stopping by woods on a snowy evening
Whose woods these are I think I know.
His house is in the village, though;
He will not see me stopping here
To watch his woods fill up with snow.

My little horse must think it queer
To stop without a farmhouse near
Between the woods and frozen lake
The darkest evening of the year.

He gives his harness bells a shake
To ask if there is some mistake.

The only other sound's the sweep
Of easy wind and downy flake.

The woods are lovely, dark, and deep,
But I have promises to keep,
And miles to go before I sleep,
And miles to go before I sleep.

Edward Thomas (1878 – 1917)

The work of Edward Thomas deserves much more popularity than it is usually given. Few other English poets wrote with such tenderness and beauty about country life and the natural world. Thomas was a somewhat reluctant poet who needed the encouragement of Robert Frost to write as he eventually did. One of the more fascinating things about his poetry is that the best of it was produced in a frenetic burst of creative energy in the last three years before he was killed in the Great War. *Old man* is, by common consent, one of his best.

Old man

Old man, or Lad's-love, in the name there's
　　nothing
To one that knows not Lad's-love, or Old
　　Man,
The hoar-green feathery herb, almost a tree,
Growing with rosemary and lavender.
Even to one that knows it well, the names
Half decorate, half perplex, the thing it is:
At least, what that is clings not to the names
In spite of time. And yet I like the names.

The herb itself I like not, but for certain
I love it, as some day the child will love it
Who plucks a feather from the door-side bush
Whenever she goes in or out of the house.
Often she waits there, snipping the tips and
    shrivelling
The shreds at last on to the path, perhaps
Thinking, perhaps of nothing, till she sniffs
Her fingers and runs off. The bush is still
But half as tall as she, though it is as old;
So well she clips it. Not a word she says;
And I can only wonder how much hereafter
She will remember, with that bitter scent,
Of garden rows, and ancient damson trees
Topping a hedge, a bent path to a door,
A low thick bush beside the door, and me
Forbidding her to pick.

                        As for myself,
Where first I met the bitter scent is lost.
I, too, often shrivel the grey shreds,
Sniff them and think and sniff again and try
Once more to think what it is I am remembering,
Always in vain. I cannot like the scent,
Yet I would rather give up others more sweet,
With no meaning, than this bitter one.

I have mislaid the key. I sniff the spray
And think of nothing; I see and hear nothing
Yet seem, too, to be listening, lying in wait
For what I should, yet never can, remember:
No garden appears, no path, no hoar-green
    bush
Of Lad's-love, or Old Man, no child beside,

Neither father nor mother, nor any playmate;
Only an avenue, dark, nameless, without end.

The sun used to shine
The sun used to shine while we two walked
Slowly together, paused and started
Again, and sometimes mused, sometimes talked
As either pleased, and cheerfully parted

Each night. We never disagreed
Which gate to rest on. The to be
And the late past we gave small heed.
We turned from men or poetry

To rumours of the war remote
Only till both stood disinclined
For aught but the yellow flavorous coat
Of an apple wasps had undermined;

Or a sentry of dark betonies,
The stateliest of small flowers on earth,
At the forest verge; or crocuses
Pale purple as if they had their birth

In sunless Hades fields. The war
Came back to mind with the moonrise
Which soldiers in the east afar
Beheld then. Nevertheless, our eyes

Could as well imagine the Crusades
Or Caesar's battles. Everything
To faintness like those rumours fades —
Like the brook's water glittering

Under the moonlight — like those walks
Now — like us two that took them, and
The fallen apples, all the talks
The silences — like memory's sand

When the tide covers it late or soon,
And other men through other flowers
In those fields under the same moon
Go talking and have easy hours.

Out in the dark
Out in the dark over the snow
The fallow fawns invisible go
With the fallow doe;
And the winds blow
Fast as the stars are slow.

Stealthily the dark haunts round
And, when the lamp goes, without sound
At a swifter bound
Than the swiftest hound,
Arrives, and all else is drowned;

And star and I and wind and deer
Are in the dark together, — near,
Yet far — and fear
Drums on my ear
In that sage company drear.

How weak and little is the light,
All the universe of sight,
Love and delight,
Before the might,
If you love it not, of night.

The owl

Downhill I came, hungry, and yet not starved;
Cold, yet had heat within me that was proof
Against the North wind; tired, yet so that rest
Had seemed the sweetest thing under a roof.

Then at the inn I had food, fire and rest,
Knowing how hungry, cold, and tired was I.
All of the night was quite barred out except
An owl's cry, a most melancholy cry

Shaken out long and clear upon the hill,
No merry note, nor cause of merriment,
But one telling me plain what I escaped
And others could not, that night, as in I went.

And salted was my food, and my repose,
Salted and sobered, too, by the bird's voice
Speaking for all who lay under the stars,
Soldiers and poor, unable to rejoice.

Adlestrop

Yes. I remember Adlestrop —
The name, because one afternoon
Of heat the express-train drew up there
Unwontedly. It was late June.

The steam hissed. Someone cleared his throat.
No one left and no one came
On the bare platform. What I saw
Was Adlestrop — only the name

And willows, willowherb, and grass,
And meadowsweet, and haycocks dry,

No whit less still and lonely fair
Than the high cloudlets in the sky.

And for that minute a blackbird sang
Close by, and round him, mistier,
Farther and farther, all the birds
Of Oxfordshire and Gloucestershire.

John Masefield (1878 – 1967)

Recognition of John Masefield's contribution
to twentieth-century poetry came when he was
made the fifteenth Poet Laureate. His most
popular works were about the sea. As a young
man he had been apprenticed as a sailor in a
windjammer which went round Cape Horn,
and memories of his life at sea never left him.

Some critics saw too much of the coarseness
of the sailor's language in his writing: others
felt he was boisterous by nature. He might
well have been, but Masefield was capable of
expressing great tenderness in his poems. *On
growing old* is a fine example.

On growing old

Be with me, Beauty, for the fire is dying.
My dog and I are old, too old for roving.
Man, whose young passion sets the spindrift
  flying,
Is soon too lame to march, too cold for
  loving.
I take the book and gather to the fire,
Turning old yellow leaves; minute by minute
The clock ticks to my heart. A withered wire,
Moves a thin ghost of music in the spinet.

I cannot sail your seas, I cannot wander
Your cornland, nor your hill-land, nor your
    valleys
Ever again, nor share the battle yonder
Where the young knight the broken squadron
    rallies.
Only stay quiet while my mind remembers
The beauty of fire from the beauty of embers.

Beauty, have pity! for the strong have power,
The rich their wealth, the beautiful their grace,
Summer of man its sunlight and its flower,
Springtime of man all April in a face.
Only, as in the jostling in the Strand,
Where the mob thrusts or loiters or is loud,
The beggar with the saucer in his hand
Asks only a penny from the passing crowd,
So, from this glittering world with all its fashion,
Its fire, and play of men, its stir, its march,
Let me have wisdom, Beauty, wisdom and passion,
Bread to the soul, rain where the summers
    parch.
Give me but these, and, though the darkness
    close,
Even the night will blossom as the rose.

Up on the Downs
Up on the downs the red-eyed kestrels hover,
Eyeing the grass.
The fieldmouse flits like a shadow into cover
As their shadows pass.

Men are burning the gorse on the down's
    shoulder;

A drift of smoke
Glitters with fire and hangs, and the skies
  smoulder,
And the lungs choke.

Once the tribe did thus on the downs, on these
  downs burning
Men in the frame.
Crying to the gods of the downs till their brains
  were turning
And the gods came.

And today on the downs, in the wind, the hawks,
  the grasses,
In blood and air,
Something passes me and cries as it passes,
On the chalk downland bare.

Cargoes
Quinquireme of Nineveh from distant Ophir
Rowing home to haven in sunny Palestine,
With a cargo of ivory,
And apes and peacocks,
Sandalwood, cedarwood, and sweet white wine.

Stately Spanish galleon coming from the Isthmus,
Dipping through the Tropics by the palm-green
  shores,
With a cargo of diamonds,
Emeralds, amethysts,
Topazes, and cinnamon, and gold moidores.

Dirty British coaster with a salt-caked smoke
  stack

Butting through the Channel in the mad March
  days,
With a cargo of Tyne coal,
Road-rail, pig-lead,
Firewood, ironware, and cheap tin trays.

Sea-fever

I must down to the seas again, to the lonely sea
  and the sky,
And all I ask is a tall ship and a star to steer
  her by,
And the wheel's kick and the wind's song and
  the white sails shaking,
And a grey mist on the sea's face and a grey
  dawn breaking.

I must down to the seas again, for the call of
  the running tide
Is a wild call and a clear call that may not be
  denied;
And all I ask is a windy day with the white
  clouds flying,
And the flung spray and the blown spume, and
  the seagulls crying.

I must down to the seas again, to the vagrant
  gypsy life,
To the gull's way and the whale's way where
  the wind's like a whetted knife;
And all I ask is a merry yarn from a laughing
  fellow-rover,
And quiet sleep and a sweet dream when the
  long trick's over.

James Elroy Flecker (1884 – 1915)

James Elroy Flecker produced an impressive body of work for one who died so young. He succumbed to tuberculosis in Switzerland at the age of 31. His career as an up-and-coming British diplomat took him to Turkey and Beirut, but poetry was his real passion. His best-known poem, *The Golden Journey to Samarkand*, owed a great deal to his fascination with all things Persian and Arabic.

All his work, some of it published after his death, is full of atmosphere. The images he employs are always vividly drawn and there is a wonderful clarity about his poems.

Santorin

(A LEGEND OF THE ÆGEAN)

'Who are you, Sea Lady,
And where in the seas are we?
I have too long been steering
By the flashes in your eyes.
Why drops the moonlight through my heart,
And why so quietly
Go the great engines of my boat
As if their souls were free?'
'Oh ask me not, bold sailor;
Is not your ship a magic ship
That sails without a sail:
Are not these isles the Isles of Greece
And dust upon the sea?
But answer me three questions
And give me answers three.
What is your ship?' 'A British.'
'And where may Britain be?'

'Oh, it lies north, dear lady;
It is a small country.'
'Yet you will know my lover
Though you live far away:
And you will whisper where he has gone,
That lily boy to look upon
And whiter than the spray.'
'How should I know your lover,
Lady of the sea?'
'Alexander, Alexander,
The King of the World was he.'
'Weep not for him, dear lady,
But come aboard my ship
So many years ago he died,
He's dead as dead can be.'
'O base and brutal sailor
To lie this lie to me,
His mother was the foam-foot
Star-sparkling Aphrodite;
His father was Adonis
Who lives away in Lebanon,
In stony Lebanon, where blooms
His red anemone.
But where is Alexander,
The soldier Alexander,
My golden love of olden days
The King of the world and me?'

She sank into the moonlight
And the sea was only sea.

Oxford Canal
When you have wearied of the valiant spires of
   this County Town,

Of its wide white streets and glistening museums,
  and black monastic walls,
Of its red motors and lumbering trams, and
  self-sufficient people,
I will take you walking with me to a place you
  have not seen —
Half town and half country — the land of the
  Canal.
It is dearer to me than the antique town: I love
  it more than the rounded hills:
Straightest, sublimest of rivers is the long
  Canal.
I have observed great storms and trembled: I
  have wept for fear of the dark.
But nothing makes me so afraid as the clear
  water of this idle canal on a summer's noon.
Do you see the great telephone poles down in
  the water, how every wire is distinct?
If a body fell into the canal it would rest
  entangled in those wires for ever, between
  earth and air.
For the water is as deep as the stars are high.

One day I was thinking how if a man fell from
  that lofty pole
He would rush through the water toward me till
  his image was scattered by his splash,
When suddenly a train rushed by: the brazen
  dome of the engine flashed: the long white
  carriages roared;
The sun veiled himself for a moment, and the
  signals loomed in fog;
A savage woman screamed at me from a barge:
  little children began to cry;

The untidy landscape rose to life; a sawmill
    started;
A cart rattled down to the wharf, and workmen
    clanged over the iron footbridge;
A beautiful old man nodded from the first-storey
    window of a square red house,
And a pretty girl came out to hang up clothes
    in a small delightful garden.
O strange motion in the suburb of a county
    town:
Slow regular movement of the dance of death!
Men and not phantoms are these that move
    in light.
Forgotten they live, and forgotten die.

From **The Golden Journey to Samarkand**
PROLOGUE
We who with songs beguile your pilgrimage
And swear that Beauty lives though lilies die,
We Poets of the proud old lineage
Who sing to find your hearts, we know not
why,

What shall we tell you? Tales, marvellous tales
Of ships and stars and isles where good men
    rest,
Where nevermore the rose of sunset pales,
And winds and shadows fall towards the West:

And there the world's first huge white-bearded
    kings
In dim glades sleeping, murmur in their sleep,
And closer round their breasts the ivy clings,
Cutting its pathway slow and red and deep.

II

And how beguile you? Death has no repose
Warmer and deeper than that Orient sand
Which hides the beauty and bright faith of
    those
Who made the Golden Journey to Samarkand.

And now they wait and whiten peaceably,
Those conquerors, those poets, those so fair:
They know time comes, not only you and I,
But the whole world shall whiten, here or
    there;

When those long caravans that cross the plain
With dauntless feet and sound of silver bells
Put forth no more for glory or for gain,
Take no more solace from the palm-girt wells.

When the great markets by the sea shut fast
All that calm Sunday that goes on and on:
When even lovers find their peace at last,
And Earth is but a star, that once had shone.

D. H. Lawrence (1885 – 1930)

D. H. Lawrence's career was forever steeped
in controversy of one sort or another, but
nothing could prevent his rise to prominence
as one of the great literary figures of the
twentieth century. His output was prodigious.
The author of *Lady Chatterley's Lover* and
Women in Love was also an indefatigable
writer of letters on a wide range of subjects,
and also wrote drama, criticism, travel books
and translations.

His reputation was largely built on his work as a novelist. Yet he was passionate about poetry. He wrote it with exuberance and verve and with torrents of creative energy. He openly admitted that the driving force for all this was his fondness for the youthfulness of America and the New World, although he was actually writing about a spirit much more elusive than any country. Lawrence admired Walt Whitman. He never achieved Whitman's technical precision or brilliance, but his stature as a poet has continued to grow long after his death. One obvious reason for this is that Lawrence wrote with great honesty and was never ashamed about exposing raw emotion.

Renascence
We have bit no forbidden apple,
Eve and I,
Yet the splashes of day and night
Falling round us, no longer dapple
The same valley with purple and white.
This is our own still valley
Our Eden, our home;
But days show it vivid with feeling,
And the pallor of night does not tally
With dark sleep that once covered the ceiling.

The little red heifer: tonight I looked in her
  eyes;
She will calve tomorrow.
Last night, when I went with the lantern, the
  sow was grabbing her litter
With snarling red jaws; and I heard the cries

Of the newborn, and then the old owl, then the
  bats that flitter.

And I woke to the sound of the woodpigeon,
  and lay and listened
Till I could borrow
A few quick beats from a woodpigeon's heart:
  and when I did rise
Saw where morning sun on the shaken iris
  glistened.
And I knew that home, this valley, was wider
  than Paradise.

I learned it all from my Eve,
The warm, dumb wisdom;
She's a quicker instructress than years;
She has quickened my pulse to receive
Strange throbs, beyond laughter and tears.

So now I know the valley
Fleshed all like me
With feelings that change and quiver
And clash, and yet seem to tally,
Like all the clash of a river
Moves on to the sea.

Piano
Softly, in the dusk, a woman is singing to me;
Taking me back down the vista of years, till
  I see
A child sitting under the piano, in the boom of
  the tingling strings,
And pressing the small, poised feet of a mother
  who smiles as she sings.

In spite of myself, the insidious mastery of song
Betrays me back, till the heart of me weeps to
  belong
To the old Sunday evenings at home, with
  winter outside
And hymns in the cosy parlour, the tinkling
  piano our guide.

So now it is vain for the singer to burst into
  clamour
With the great black piano appassionato. The
  glamour
Of childish days is upon me, my manhood
  is cast
Down in the flood of·remembrance, I weep like
  a child for the past.

Humbert Wolfe (1886 – 1940)

Wolfe was an under-secretary in the Ministry
of Labour in the 1930s who also managed to
write some pithy epigrams. *Over the fire* is
typically blunt and witty.

From **The uncelestial city, Bk.I ii. 2.**
Over the fire
You cannot hope
  to bribe or twist,
thank God! the
  British journalist.

But, seeing what
  the man will do
unbribed, there's
  no occasion to.

Roy Campbell (1902 – 57)

Campbell was a South African poet who produced a notable translation of Baudelaire's *Les fleurs du mal*. The short poem included here should be required reading for all writers.

On some South African novelists

You praise the firm restraint with which they
    write —
I'm with you there, of course:
They use the snaffle and the bit all right,
But where's the bloody horse?

Rupert Brooke (1887 – 1915)

Rupert Brooke's reputation was probably never as high as in the years immediately after his death. He had been praised as 'all that one could wish England's noblest sons to be' and described by a contemporary as: 'A Young Apollo, golden-haired, /Magnificently unprepared/ For the long littleness of life.'

This was almost inevitably followed by the criticism that his work was too stridently patriotic. Time has chipped away at both extremes, and Brooke is now admired as a poet who wrote passionately, with affection and humanity. He was a complex man who discovered a literary style of quiet elegance. One approaches his work with unrestrained delight.

Rupert Brooke published his first volume of poetry in 1911 and died only four years later at the age of 28. But he devoted so much of his life to poetry, that he became the poet's poet. Recognition of his brilliance centred at first on his *War Sonnets*. The reputation of the *Sonnets* partly obscured the fact that Brooke wrote about other subjects, with genuine emotion, and tenderness and with a maturity that went far beyond his years.

Heaven

Fish (fly-replete, in depth of June,
Dawdling away their watery noon)
Ponder deep wisdom, dark or clear,
Each secret fishy hope or fear.
Fish say, they have their Stream and Pond;
But is there anything Beyond?
This life cannot be All, they swear,
For how unpleasant if it were!
One may not doubt that, somehow, Good
Shall come of Water and of Mud;
And, sure, the reverent eye must see
A Purpose in Liquidity.
We darkly know, by Faith we cry,
The future is not Wholly Dry.
Mud unto mud! — Death eddies near —
Not here the appointed End, not here!
But somewhere, beyond Space and Time,
Is wetter water, slimier slime!
And there, (they trust) there swimmeth One
Who swam ere rivers were begun,
Immense, of fishy form and mind,
Squamous, omnipotent, and kind;
And under that Almighty Fin,
The littlest fish may enter in.
Oh! never fly conceals a hook,
Fish say, in the Eternal Brook,

But more than mundane weeds are there,
And mud, celestially fair;
Fat caterpillars drift around,
And Paradisal grubs are found;
Unfading moths, immortal flies,
And the worm that never dies.
And in that Heaven of all their wish,
There shall be no more land, say fish.

The hill
Breathless, we flung us on the windy hill,
Laughed in the sun, and kissed the lovely
    grass.
You said, 'Through glory and ecstasy we pass;
Wind, sun and earth remain, the birds sing
    still,
When we are old, are old . . . ' 'And when
    we die
All's over that is ours; and life burns on
Through other lovers, other lips,' said I,
'Heart of my heart, our heaven is now, is
    won!'

'We are Earth's best, that learnt her lesson
    here.
Life is our cry. We have kept the faith!' we
    said;
'We shall go down with unreluctant tread
Rose-crowned into the darkness!' . . . Proud
    we were,
And laughed, that had such brave true things
    to say.
— And then you suddenly cried, and turned
    away.

Finding

From the candles and dumb shadows,
And the house where love had died.
I stole to the vast moonlight
And the whispering life outside.
But I found no lips of comfort,
No home in the moon's light
(I, little and lone and frightened
In the unfriendly night),
And no meaning in the voices . . .
Far over the lands, and through
The dark, beyond the ocean,
I willed to think of you!
For I knew, had you been with me
I'd have known the words of night,
Found peace of heart, gone gladly
In comfort of that light.
Oh! the wind with soft beguiling
Would have stolen my thought away
And the night, subtly smiling,
Came by the silver way;
And the moon came down and danced to me,
And her robe was white and flying;
And trees bent their heads to me
Mysteriously crying;
And dead voices wept around me;
And dead soft fingers thrilled;
And the little gods whispered . . .
  But ever
Desperately I willed;
Till all grew soft and far
And silent . . .
  And suddenly
I found you white and radiant,

Sleeping quietly,
Far out through the tides of darkness,
And I there in that great light
Was alone, no more, nor fearful;
For there, in the homely night,
Was no thought else that mattered,
And nothing else was true,
But the white fire of moonlight,
And a white dream of you.

Retrospect

In your arms was still delight,
Quiet as a street at night;
And thoughts of you, I do remember,
Were green leaves in a darkened chamber,
Were dark clouds in a moonless sky.
Love, in you, went passing by,
Penetrative, remote, and rare,
Like a bird in the wide air,
And, as the bird, it left no trace
In the heaven of your face.

In your stupidity I found
The sweet hush after a sweet sound.
All about you was the light
That dims the greying end of night;
Desire was the unrisen sun,
Joy, the day not yet begun,
With tree whispering to tree,
Without wind, quietly.
Wisdom slept within your hair,
And Long-Suffering was there.

And in the flowing of your dress,
Undiscerning Tenderness.
And when you thought, it seemed to me,
Infinitely, and like a sea,
About the slight world you had known
Your vast unconciousness was thrown . . .

O haven without wave or tide!
Silence, in which all songs have died!
Holy book, where hearts are still!
And home at length under the hill!
O mother-quiet, breasts of peace,
Where love itself would faint and cease!
O infinite deep I never knew,
I would come back, come back to you,
Find you, as a pool unstirred,
Kneel down by you, and never a word,
Lay my head, and nothing said,
In your hands, ungarlanded;
And a long watch you would keep;
And I should sleep, and I should sleep!

The soldier
If I should die, think only this of me:
    That there's some corner of a foreign field
That is for ever England. There shall be
    In that rich earth a richer dust concealed;
A dust whom England bore, shaped, made
    aware,
    Gave, once, her flowers to love, her ways to
    roam,
A body of England's, breathing English air,
    Washed by the rivers, blest by suns of home.

And think, this heart, all evil shed away,
  A pulse in the eternal mind, no less
    Gives somewhere back the thoughts by
  England given;
Her sights and sounds; dreams happy as her
  day;
  And laughter, learnt of friends; and gentleness,
    In hearts at peace, under an English heaven.

T. S. Eliot (1888 – 1965)

Whenever I pick up an anthology of modern verse, I invariably turn to the works of T. S. Eliot. His poetry is for reading aloud, even if to oneself. And in the act of doing that, there are frequent pauses to savour words and thoughts which resonate with profundity, power, and with stunning beauty.

Eliot is the absolute master of twentieth-century verse. His work shines with a technical brilliance that lights up the mind and never fails to give the sweetest pleasure.

Eyes that last I saw in tears

Eyes that last I saw in tears
Through division
Here in death's dream kingdom
The golden vision reappears
I see the eyes but not the tears
This is my affliction

This is my affliction
Eyes I shall not see again
Eyes of decision
Eyes I shall not see unless

223

At the door of death's other kingdom
Where, as in this,
The eyes outlast a little while
A little while outlast the tears
And hold us in derision.

Sweeney among the nightingales

Apeneck Sweeney spreads his knees
Letting his arms hang down to laugh,
The zebra stripes along his jaw
Swelling to maculate giraffe.

The circles of the stormy moon
Slide westward toward the River Plate,
Death and the Raven drift above
And Sweeney guards the hornèd gate.

Gloomy Orion and the Dog
Are veiled; and hushed the shrunken seas;
The person in the Spanish cape
Tries to sit on Sweeney's knees.

Slips and pulls the table cloth
Overturns a coffee-cup,
Reorganised upon the floor
She yawns and draws a stocking up;

The silent man in mocha brown
Sprawls at the window-sill and gapes;
The waiter brings in oranges
Bananas figs and hothouse grapes;

The silent vertebrate in brown
Contracts and concentrates, withdraws;

Rachel *née* Rabinovitch
Tears at the grapes with murderous paws;

She and the lady in the cape
Are suspect, thought to be in league;
Therefore the man with heavy eyes
Declines the gambit, shows fatigue,

Leaves the room and reappears
Outside the window, leaning in,
Branches of wistaria
Circumscribe a golden grin;

The host with someone indistinct
Converses at the door apart,
The nightingales are singing near
The convent of the Sacred Heart,

And sang within the bloody wood
When Agamemnon cried aloud,
And let their liquid siftings fall
To stain the stiff dishonoured shroud.

Wilfred Owen (1893 – 1918)
Throughout the centuries, poems about war
have moved from the glorification of the art of
conflict to a recognition of its senseless
brutality and its appalling inhumanity.

Wilfred Owen's work encapsulated all that
and more. He wrote movingly about the
passion and the wastefulness, the heroism and
the tragedy.

He was only 25 when he was killed in
action.

The send-off

Down the close, darkening lanes they sang
   their way
To the siding-shed,
And lined the train with faces grimly gay.

Their breasts were stuck all white with wreath
   and spray
As men's are, dead.

Dull porters watched them, and a casual tramp
Stood staring hard,
Sorry to miss them from the upland camp.
Then, unmoved, signals nodded, and a lamp
Winked to the guard.

So secretly, like wrongs hushed-up, they went.
They were not ours:
We never heard to which front these were sent.

Nor if they yet mock what women meant
Who gave them flowers.

Shall they return to beatings of great bells
In wild train-loads?
A few, a few, too few for drums and yells,

May creep back, silent, to village wells
Up half-known roads.

Strange meeting

It seemed that out of battle I escaped
Down some profound dull tunnel, long since
   scooped

Through granites which titanic wars had
  groined.
Yet also there encumbered sleepers groaned,
Too fast in thought or death to be bestirred.
Then, as I probed them, one sprang up and
  stared
With piteous recognition in fixed eyes,
Lifting distressful hands as if to bless.
And by his smile I knew that sullen hall,
By his dead smile I knew we stood in Hell.
With a thousand pains that vision's face was
  grained;
Yet no blood reached there from the upper
  ground,
And no guns thumped, or down the flues made
  moan.
'Strange friend,' I said, 'here is no cause to
  mourn.'
'None,' said the other, 'save the undone years,
The hopelessness. Whatever hope is yours,
Was my life also; I went hunting wild
After the wildest beauty in the world,
Which lies not calm in eyes, or braided hair,
But mocks the steady running of the hour,
And if it grieves, grieves richlier than here.
For of my glee might many men have laughed,
And of my weeping something had been left,
Which must die now. I mean the truth untold,
The pity of war, the pity war distilled.
Now men will go content with what we spoiled,
Or, discontent, boil bloody, and be spilled.
They will be swift with swiftness of the tigress,
None will break ranks, though nations trek from
  progress.

Courage was mine, and I had mystery,
Wisdom was mine, and I had mastery;
To miss the march of this retreating world
Into vain citadels that are not walled.
Then, when much blood had clogged their
    chariot wheels,
I would go up and wash them from sweet
    wells,
Even with truths that lie too deep for taint.
I would have poured my spirit without stint
But not through wounds; not on the cess of
    war.
Foreheads of men have bled where no wounds
    were.
I am the enemy you killed, my friend.
I knew you in this dark; for so you frowned
Yesterday through me as you jabbed and killed.
I parried; but my hands were loath and cold.
Let us sleep now . . . '

Conscious
His fingers wake, and flutter; up the bed.
His eyes come open with a pull of will,
Helped by the yellow May-flowers by his head.
The blind-cord drawls across the window-sill . . .
What a smooth floor the ward has! What
    a rug!
Who is that talking somewhere out of sight?
Why are they laughing? What's inside that jug?
'Nurse! Doctor!' — 'Yes; all right, all right.'

But sudden evening muddles all the air —
There seems no time to want a drink of water,
Nurse looks so far away. And here and there

228

Music and roses burst through crimson slaughter.
He can't remember where he saw blue sky.
More blankets. Cold. He's cold. And yet so
   hot.
And there's no light to see the voices by;
There is no time to ask — he knows not what.

Futility
Move him into the sun —
Gently its touch awoke him once,
At home, whispering of fields unsown.
Always it woke him, even in France,
Until this morning and this snow.
If anything might rouse him now
The kind old sun will know.

Think how it wakes the seeds, —
Woke, once, the clays of a cold star.
Are limbs, so dear-achieved, are sides,
Full-nerved — still warm — too hard to stir?
Was it for this the clay grew tall?
— O what made fatuous sunbeams toil
To break earth's sleep at all?

e. e. cummings (1894 – 1962)
cummings was born in Cambridge,
Massachusetts, and was educated at the local
college which happened to be Harvard. His
poetry was initially noted for its lack of
capitalisation, but cummings was strong on
content as well as form. In *plato told*, the
'nipponized bit of the old sixth avenue el'
alludes to the Japanese bombs which fell on
Pearl Harbor in 1941.

plato told
Plato told

him:he couldn't
believe it(jesus

told him;he
wouldn't believe
it)lao

tsze
certainly told
him, and general
(yes

mam)
sherman;
and even
(believe it
or

not)you
told him:i told
him;we told him
(he didn't believe it,no

sir)it took
a nipponized bit of
the old sixth
avenue
el;in the top of his head:to tell

him

230

'but why should'
'but why should'

the
greatest
of

living magicians (whom

you and i
some
times call

april)must often

have wondered
'most

people be quite

so(when flowers)in
credibly
(always are beautiful)

ugly'

anyone lived in a pretty how town
anyone lived in a pretty how town
(with up so floating many bells down)
spring summer autumn winter
he sang his didn't he danced his did.

Women and men (both little and small)
cared for anyone not at all

they sowed their isn't they reaped their same
sun moon stars rain

children guessed (but only a few
and down they forgot as up they grew
autumn winter spring summer)
that noone loved him more by more

when by now and tree by leaf
she laughed his joy she cried his grief
bird by snow and stir by still
anyone's any was all to her

someones married their everyones
laughed their cryings and did their dance
(sleep wake hope and then)they
said their nevers they slept their dream

stars rain sun moon
(and only the snow can begin to explain
how children are apt to forget to remember
with up so floating many bells down)

one day anyone died i guess
(and noone stopped to kiss his face)
busy folk buried them side by side
little by little and was by was

all by all and deep by deep
and more by more they dream their sleep
noone and anyone earth by april
wish by spirit and if by yes.

Women and men(both dong and ding)
summer autumn winter spring
reaped their sowing and went their came
sun moon stars rain

Robert Graves (1895 – 1985)
A Londoner, Graves joined the army in 1914
and began publishing poetry while serving in
the Great War. Although Graves thought of
himself as a poet, his prose, especially
Goodbye to all that, was equally well received.
Graves and his second wife settled in the
Mallorcan village of Deya in 1946. There he
produced many volumes of poetry, amongst
other works, whilst enjoying an often eccentric
lifestyle. He is buried in the tiny church
graveyard in Deya, where the inscription on
the small tombstone reads: *Roberto Graves
Poeta*.

Full moon
As I walked out that sultry night,
  I heard the stroke of one.
The moon, attained to her full height,
  Stood beaming like the sun:
She exorcised the ghostly wheat
To mute assent in love's defeat,
  Whose tryst had now begun.

The fields lay sick beneath my tread,
  A tedious owlet cried,
A nightingale above my head
  With this or that replied —
Like man and wife who nightly keep

Inconsequent debate in sleep
  As they dream side by side.

Your phantom wore the moon's cold mask,
  My phantom wore the same;
Forgetful of the feverish task
  In hope of which they came,
Each image held the other's eyes
And watched a grey distraction rise
  To cloud the eager flame —

To cloud the eager flame of love,
  To fog the shining gate;
They held the tyrannous queen above
  Sole mover of their fate,
They glared as marble statues glare
Across the tessellated stair
  Or down the halls of state.

And now warm earth was Arctic sea,
  Each breath came dagger-keen;
Two bergs of glinting ice were we,
  The broad moon sailed between;
There swam the mermaids, tailed and finned,
And love went by upon the wind
  As though it had not been.

It was all very tidy
When I reached his place,
The grass was smooth,
The wind was delicate,
The wit well timed,
The limbs well formed,

234

The pictures straight on the wall:
It was all very tidy.

He was cancelling out
The last row of figures,
He had his beard tied up in ribbons,
There was no dust on his shoe,
Everyone nodded:
It was all very tidy.

Music was not playing,
There were no sudden noises,
The sun shone blandly,
The clock ticked:
It was all very tidy.

'Apart from and above all this,'
I reassured myself,
'There is now myself.'
It was all very tidy.

Death did not address me,
He had nearly done:
It was all very tidy.

They asked, did I not think
It was all very tidy?

I could not bring myself
To laugh, or untie
His beard's neat ribbons,
Or jog his elbow,
Or whistle, or sing,
Or make disturbance.

I consented, frozenly,
He was unexceptionable.
It was all very tidy.

Nature's lineaments
When mountain rocks and leafy trees
And clouds and things like these,
With edges,

Caricature the human face,
Such scribblings have no grace
Nor peace —

The bulbous nose, the sunken chin,
The ragged mouth in grin
Of cretin.

Nature is always so: you find
That all she has of mind
Is wind,

Retching among the empty spaces,
Ruffling the idiot grasses,
The sheep's fleeces.

Whose pleasures are excreting, poking,
Havocking and sucking,
Sleepy licking.

Whose griefs are melancholy,
Whose flowers are oafish,
Whose waters, silly,
Whose birds, raffish,
Whose fish, fish.

Basil Bunting (1900 – 85)
Although born in Northumberland, Bunting,
despite success abroad, did not make an
impact in Britain until late in his life. In
What the chairman told Tom, Bunting speaks
for poets of every age.

What the chairman told Tom
Poetry? It's a hobby.
I run model trains.
Mr Shaw there breeds pigeons.

It's not work. You don't sweat.
Nobody pays for it.
You *could* advertise soap.

Art, that's opera; or repertory —
The Desert Song.
Nancy was in the chorus.

But to ask for twelve pounds a week —
married, aren't you? —
you've got a nerve.

How could I look a bus conductor
in the face
if I paid you twelve pounds?

Who says it's poetry, anyhow?
My ten-year-old
can do it *and* rhyme.

I get three thousand and expenses,
a car, vouchers,
but I'm an accountant.

They do what I tell them,
my company.
What do *you* do?

Nasty little words, nasty long words,
it's unhealthy.
I want to wash when I meet a poet.

They're Reds, addicts,
all delinquents.
What you write is rot.

Mr Hines says so, and he's a schoolteacher,
he ought to know.
Go and find *work*.

A. S. J. Tessimond (1902 – 62)

There is something vibrant about West Indian
poetry. Once, West Indian poets drew
inspiration from the history of the islands and
from their colonial mainsprings. Now they
immerse themselves in the flourish of
contemporary local life and their work is
ingeniously woven around the hopes and
aspirations of people in a new and emerging
world. Almost everything written in this genre
is wonderfully descriptive, and full of the life
and verve of the region. A. S. J. Tessimond's
view of a Jamaican bus ride, in which his

readers are invited to share the excitement of
a routine journey, is typical.

Jamaican bus ride

The live fowl squatting on the grapefruit and
    bananas
in the basket of the copper-coloured lady is
    gloomy but resigned.
The four very large baskets on the floor
are in everybody's way,
as the conductor points out
loudly, often, but in vain.

Two quadroon dandies are disputing
who is standing on whose feet.

When we stop,
a boy vanishes through the door marked
    ENTRANCE;
but those entering through the door marked
    EXIT
are greatly hindered by the fact that when we
    started
there were twenty standing
and another ten have somehow inserted themselves
into invisible crannies
between dark sweating body and body.

With an odour of petrol
both excessive and alarming
we hurtle hell-for-leather
between crimson bougainvillaea blossom
and scarlet poinsettia
and miraculously do not run over

239

three goats, seven hens and a donkey
as we pray
that the driver has not fortified himself
at Daisy's Drinking Saloon
with more than four rums:
or by the gods of Jamaica
this day is our last!

A hot day
Cottonwool clouds loiter.
A lawnmower, very far,
Birrs. Then a bee comes
To a crimson rose and softly,
Deftly and fatly crams
A velvet body in.

A tree, June-lazy, makes
A tent of dim green light.
Sunlight weaves in the leaves,
Honey-light laced with leaf-light,
Green interleaved with gold.
Sunlight gathers its rays
In sheaves, which the wind unweaves
And then reweaves — the wind
That puffs a smell of grass
Through the heat — heavy, trembling
Summer pool of air.

Cats II
Cats, no less liquid than their shadows,
Offer no angles to the wind.
They slip, diminished, neat, through loopholes
Less than themselves; will not be pinned

To rules or routes for journeys; counter
Attack with non-resistance; twist
Enticing through the curving fingers
And leave an angered, empty fist.

They wait obsequious as darkness —
Quick to retire, quick to return;
Admit no aim or ethics; flatter
With reservations; will not learn

To answer to their names; are seldom
Truly owned till shot and skinned.
Cats, no less liquid than their shadows,
Offer no angles to the wind.

If men were not striped like tigers

How much simpler if men were not striped like
    tigers, patched like clowns;
If alternate white and black were not further
    confused by greys and browns;
If people were, even at times, consistent wholes;
If the actors were rigidly typed and kept their
    roles;
If we were able
To classify friends, each with his label,
Each label neat
As the names of cakes or the categories of
    meat.
But you, my dear, are a greedy bitch, yet also
    a sad child lost,
And you who have swindled your partners are
    kind to the cat,
And, in human beings, this is not this nor that
    quite that

And the threads are crossed
And nothing's as tidy as the mind could wish
And the human mammal is partly insect and
    often reptile and also fish.

Pablo Neruda (1904 – 73)

Pablo Neruda, the Chilean poet, was one of
the towering figures of contemporary literature.
His work has frequently been compared to
Walt Whitman's because of the grand sweep
of its emotions and its concern with the
human condition. His poems were always very
political, but that was only because the people
were so important — especially the poor and
the dispossessed.

Once, when shown some magnificent
ancient ruins, his interest immediately turned
to 'the hands that built them'. Yet as a poet,
Neruda is wildly romantic, and wonderful to
read.

Sonata and destructions

After so many things, after so many hazy miles,
not sure which kingdom it is, not knowing the
    terrain,
travelling with pitiful hopes,
and lying companions, and suspicious dreams,
I love the firmness that still survives in my
    eyes,
I hear my heart beating as if I were riding a
    horse,
I bite the sleeping fire and the ruined salt,
and at night, when darkness is thick, and
    mourning furtive,

242

I imagine I am the one keeping watch on the
   far shore
of the encampments, the traveller armed
with his sterile defences,
caught between growing shadows
and shivering wings, and my arm made of stone
   protects me.
There's a confused altar among the sciences
   of tears,
and in my twilight meditations with no perfume,
and in my deserted sleeping rooms where the
   moon lives,
and the spiders that belong to me, and the
   destructions I am fond of.
I love my own lost self, my faulty stuff,
my silver wound, and my eternal loss.
The damp grapes burned, and their funeral
   water
is still flickering, is still with us,
and the sterile inheritance, and the treacherous
   home.
Who performed a ceremony of ashes?

Who loved the lost thing, who sheltered the last
   thing of all?
The father's bone, the dead ship's timber,
   and his own end, his flight,
his melancholy power, his god that had bad luck?

I lie in wait, then, for what is not alive and
   what is suffering,
and the extraordinary testimony I bring forward,
with brutal efficiency and written down in ashes,
is the form of oblivion that I prefer,

the name I give to the earth, the value of my
    dreams,
the endless abundance which I distribute
with my wintry eyes, every day this world goes
    on.

Sir John Betjeman (1906 – 84)

Sir John Betjeman, who was made Poet
Laureate in 1972, revelled in the thorough
Englishness of his work. He wrote about his
English passions, such as old churches and
railways, with profound love and caring and
with beautiful simplicity.

He held firm views about the rapidly
changing world and did not believe that we
were always making real progress in such
fields as architecture. We are fortunate to have
heard him talk on radio and on television
about his poetry, frequently with a twinkle in
his eye and a delicious sense of mischief. I've
always felt that there is a great deal of that in
A Subaltern's love-song.

A Subaltern's love-song

Miss J. Hunter Dunn, Miss J. Hunter Dunn,
Furnish'd and burnish'd by Aldershot sun,
What strenuous singles we played after tea,
We in the tournament — you against me!

Love-thirty, love-forty, oh! weakness of joy,
The speed of a swallow, the grace of a boy,
With carefullest carelessness, gaily you won,
I am weak from your loveliness, Joan Hunter
    Dunn.

Miss Joan Hunter Dunn, Miss Joan Hunter
Dunn
How mad I am, sad I am, glad that you won.
The warm-handled racket is back in its press,
But my shock-headed victor, she loves me no
less.

Her father's euonymus shines as we walk,
And swing past the summer-house, buried in
talk,
And cool the verandah that welcomes us in
To the six-o'clock news and a lime-juice and
gin.

The scent of the conifers, sound of the bath,
The view from my bedroom of moss-dappled
path,
As I struggle with double-end evening tie,
For we dance at the Golf-Club, my victor
and I.

On the floor of her bedroom lie blazer and
shorts
And the cream-coloured walls are be-trophied
with sports,
And westering, questioning settles the sun
On your low-leaded window, Miss Joan Hunter
Dunn.

The Hillman is waiting, the light's in the hall,
The pictures of Egypt are bright on the wall,
My sweet, I am standing beside the oak stair
And there on the landing's the light on your
hair.

By roads 'not adopted', by woodlanded ways,
She drove to the club in the late summer
  haze,
Into nine-o'clock Camberley, heavy with bells.
And mushroomy, pine-woody, evergreen smells.

Miss Joan Hunter Dunn, Miss Joan Hunter
  Dunn,
I can hear from the car park the dance has
  begun.
Oh! full Surrey twilight! importunate band!
Oh! strongly adorable tennis-girl's hand!

Around us are Rovers and Austins afar,
Above us, the intimate roof of the car,
And here on my right is the girl of my choice,
With the tilt of her nose and the chime of her
  voice,

And the scent of her wrap, and the words
  never said,
And the ominous, ominous dancing ahead.
We sat in the car park till twenty to one
And now I'm engaged to Miss Joan Hunter
  Dunn.

Seaside golf
How straight it flew, how long it flew,
It clear'd the rutty track
And soaring, disappeared from view
Beyond the bunker's back —
A glorious, sailing, bounding drive
That made me glad I was alive.

And down the fairway, far along
It glowed a lonely white;
I played an iron sure and strong
And clipp'd it out of sight,
And spite of grassy banks between
I knew I'd find it on the green.

And so I did. It lay content
Two paces from the pin;
A steady putt and then it went
Oh, most securely in.
The very turf rejoiced to see
That quite unprecedented three.

Ah! seaweed smells from sandy caves
And thyme and mist in whiffs,
Incoming tide, Atlantic waves
Slapping the sunny cliffs,
Lark song and sea sounds in the air
And splendour, splendour everywhere.

Death in Leamington
She dies in the upstairs bedroom
By the light of the ev'ning star
That shone through the plate glass window
From over Leamington Spa.

Beside her the lonely crochet
Lay patiently and unstirred,
But the fingers that would have work'd it
Were dead as the spoken word.

And Nurse came in with the tea-things
Breast high 'mid the stands and chairs —

But Nurse was alone with her own little soul,
And the things were alone with theirs.

She bolted the big round window,
She let the blinds unroll,
She set a match to the mantle,
She covered the fire with coal.

And 'Tea!' she said in a tiny voice
'Wake up! It's nearly *five*.'
Oh! Chintzy, chintzy cheeriness,
Half dead and half alive!

Do you know that the stucco is peeling?
Do you know that the heart will stop?
From those yellow Italianate arches
Do you hear the plaster drop?

Nurse looked at the silent bedstead,
At the grey, decaying face,
As the calm of a Leamington ev'ning
Drifted into the place.

She moved the table of bottles
Away from the bed to the wall;
And tiptoeing gently over the stairs
Turned down the gas in the hall.

W. H. Auden (1907 – 73)
I fell in love with Auden's *Lullaby* from the
moment I read it first. I am no authority on
his work, but he would have written few
things more structurally perfect. There is a
compelling and haunting beauty about it.

The immense pleasure we get from reading Auden's poems today can be explained partly by the fact that he was a man of our time who felt thoroughly at home writing in our century. His themes were universal but they had so much relevance to the age in which he lived that he became an instant success. Few English poets achieved fame so rapidly. America and the Church altered his style in the 1940s, but his work retained its beauty and its passion. He wrote the most celebrated love lyric of our time: 'Lay your sleeping head, my love/ Human on my faithless arm' and from the film *Four Weddings and a Funeral* we know the powerful emotions his work evokes today.

Lullaby
Lay your sleeping head, my love,
Human on my faithless arm;
Time and fevers burn away
Individual beauty from
Thoughtful children, and the grave
Proves the child ephemeral:
But in my arms till break of day
Let the living creature lie,
Mortal, guilty, but to me
The entirely beautiful.

Soul and body have no bounds:
To lovers as they lie upon
Her tolerant enchanted slope
In their ordinary swoon,
Grave the vision Venus sends

Of supernatural sympathy,
Universal love and hope;
While an abstract insight wakes
Among the glaciers and the rocks
The hermit's carnal ecstasy.

Certainty, fidelity
On the stroke of midnight pass
Like vibrations of a bell
And fashionable madmen raise
Their pedantic boring cry:
Every farthing of the cost,
All the dreaded cards foretell,
Shall be paid, but from this night
Not a whisper, not a thought,
Not a kiss nor look be lost.

Beauty, midnight, vision dies:
Let the winds of dawn that blow
Softly round your dreaming head
Such a day of welcome show
Eye and knocking heart may bless,
Find our mortal world enough;
Noons of dryness find you fed
By the involuntary powers,
Nights of insult let you pass
Watched by every human love.

The Crossroads
The friends who met here and embraced are
    gone,
Each to his own mistake; one flashes on
To fame and ruin in a rowdy lie,
A village torpor holds the other one,

Some local wrong where it takes time to die;
The empty junction glitters in the sun.
So at all quays and crossroads: who can tell,
O places of decision and farewell,
To what dishonour all adventure leads,
What parting gift could give that friend
    protection,
So orientated, his salvation needs
The Bad Lands and the sinister direction?

All landscapes and all weathers freeze with
    fear,
But none have ever thought, the legends say,
The time allowed made it impossible;
For even the most pessimistic set
The limit of their errors at a year.
What friends could there be left then to betray,
What joy takes longer to atone for? Yet
Who would complete without the extra day
The journey that should take no time at all?

Musée des Beaux Arts
About suffering they were never wrong,
The Old Masters: how well they understood
Its human position; how it takes place
While someone else is eating or opening a
    window or just walking dully along;
How, when the aged are reverently, passionately
    waiting
For the miraculaous birth, there always must be
Children who did not especially want it to
    happen, skating
On a pond at the edge of the wood:
They never forgot

That even the dreadful martyrdom must run its
   course
Anyhow in a corner, some untidy spot
Where the dogs go on with their doggy life and
   the torturer's horse
Scratches its innocent behind on a tree.
In Breughel's *Icarus*, for instance: how everything
   turns away
Quite leisurely from the disaster; the ploughman
   may
Have heard the splash, the forsaken cry,
But for him it was not an important failure; the
   sun shone
As it had to on the white legs disappearing into
   the green
Water; and the expensive, delicate ship that must
   have seen
Something amazing, a boy falling out of the sky,
Had somewhere to get to and sailed calmly on.

Funeral blues (IX of Twelve poems)
Stop all the clocks, cut off the telephone,
Prevent the dog from barking with a juicy
   bone,
Silence the pianos and with muffled drum
Bring out the coffin, let the mourners come.

Let aeroplanes circle moaning overhead
Scribbling on the sky the message He Is Dead,
Put crêpe bows round the white necks of the
   public doves,
Let the traffic policemen wear black cotton
   gloves.

He was my North, my South, my East and
   West,
My working week and my Sunday rest,
My noon, my midnight, my talk, my song;
I thought that love would last for ever: I was
   wrong.

The stars are not wanted now; put out every
   one;
Pack up the moon and dismantle the sun;
Pour away the ocean and sweep up the wood;
For nothing now can ever come to any good.

Sir Stephen Spender (1909 – 95)
Spender was part of that remarkable group
which included W.H. Auden, Christopher
Isherwood and Louis MacNeice, who were at
University College, Oxford together in the
twenties. Although Spender has always been a
political activist, who preached the importance
of treating political subjects in literature, his
best poetry is very personal.

The room above the square
The light in the window seemed perpetual
Where you stayed in the high room for me;
It flowered above the trees through leaves
Like my certainty.

The light is fallen and you are hidden
In sunbright peninsulas of the sword:
Torn like leaves through Europe is the peace
Which through me flowed.

Now I climb alone to the dark room
Which hangs above the square
Where among stones and roots the other
Peaceful lovers are.

What I expected

What I expected, was
Thunder, fighting,
Long struggles with men
And climbing.
After continual straining
I should grow strong;
Then the rocks would shake
And I should rest long.

What I had not foreseen
Was the gradual day
Weakening the will
Leaking the brightness away,
The lack of good to touch
The fading of body and soul
Like smoke before wind,
Corrupt, unsubstantial.

The wearing of Time,
And the watching of cripples pass
With limbs shaped like questions
In their odd twist,
The pulverous grief
Melting the bones with pity,
The sick falling from earth —
These, I could not foresee.

For I had expected always
Some brightness to hold in trust,
Some final innocence
To save from dust;
That, hanging solid,
Would dangle through all,
Like the created poem
Or the dazzling crystal.

Dylan Thomas (1914 – 53)
There are more myths about Dylan Thomas
than almost any other poet. He would have
approved of them all, because he contributed
to their circulation. Thomas wanted to be
thought of as brilliantly successful and larger
than life, when in fact he had a weak
constitution and struggled in his career simply
to survive. He was a mass of contradictions.
He acquired the reputation of being a great
drinker although he couldn't hold his drink;
he became famous as the Welsh poet who
spoke no Welsh. His greatness comes from his
passion for and his exquisite use of the
English language, following with distinction in
the tradition of the great Romantics.

Elegy was probably the last poem that
Dylan Thomas wrote, and its final lines were
pieced together from the copious notes he left.

It is an expression of his most profound
thoughts about the death of his father, and
although its mood is slightly more resigned
than that of his poem *Do not go gentle into
that good night*, it burns with filial pride
. . . 'too proud to cry'.

255

And, of course, the music in Dylan Thomas's verse is inescapable. The words hum on the page and their sounds echo in the mind long after they are read.

Elegy

Too proud to die, broken and blind he died
The darkest way, and did not turn away,
A cold kind man brave in his narrow pride

On that darkest day. Oh, forever may
He lie lightly, at last, on the last, crossed
Hill, under the grass, in love, and there grow

Young among the long flocks, and never lie
    lost
Or still all the numberless days of his death,
    though
Above all he longed for his mother's breast

Which was rest and dust, and in the kind
    ground
The darkest justice of death, blind and
    unblessed.
Let him find no rest but be fathered and found,

I prayed in the crouching room, by his blind bed,
In the muted house, one minute before
Noon, and night, and light. The rivers of the
    dead

Veined his poor hand I held, and I saw
Through his unseeing eyes to the roots of the sea.
An old tormented man three-quarters blind,

I am not too proud to cry that He and he
Will never never go out of my mind.
All his bones crying, and poor in all but pain,

Being innocent, he dreaded that he died
Hating his God, but what he was was plain:
An old kind man brave in his burning pride.

The sticks of the house were his; his books he
  owned.
Even as a baby he had never cried;
Nor did he now, save to his secret wound.

Out of his eyes I saw the last light glide.
Here among the light of the lording sky
An old blind man is with me where I go

Walking in the meadows of his son's eye
On whom a world of ills came down like
  snow.
He cried as he died, fearing at last the spheres'

Last sound, the world going out without a
  breath:
Too proud to cry, too frail to check the tears,
And caught between two nights, blindness and
  death.

O deepest wound of all that he should die
On that darkest day. Oh, he could hide
The tears out of his eyes, too proud to cry.

Until I die he will not leave my side.

The hand that signed the paper

The hand that signed the paper felled a city;
Five sovereign fingers taxed the breath,
Doubled the globe of dead and halved a
    country;
These five kings did a king to death.

The mighty hand leads to a sloping shoulder,
The finger joints are cramped with chalk;
A goose's quill has put an end to murder
That put an end to talk.

The hand that signed the treaty bred a fever,
And famine grew, and locusts came;
Great is the hand that holds dominion over
Man by a scribbled name.

The five kings count the dead but do not
    soften
The crusted wound nor stroke the brow;
A hand rules pity as a hand rules heaven;
Hands have no tears to flow.

Do not go gentle into that good night

Do not go gentle into that good night,
Old age should burn and rave at close of day;
Rage, rage against the dying of the light.

Though wise men at their end know dark
    is right,
Because their words had forked no lightning
    they
Do not go gentle into that good night.

Good men, the last wave by, crying how
   bright
Their frail deeds might have danced in a green
   bay,
Rage, rage against the dying of the light.

Wild men who caught and sang the sun in
   flight,
And learn, too late, they grieved it on its way,
Do not go gentle into that good night.

Grave men, near death, who see with blinding
   sight
Blind eyes could blaze like meteors and be
   gay,
Rage, rage against the dying of the light.

And you, my father, there on the sad height,
Curse, bless, me now with your fierce tears,
   I pray.
Do not go gentle into that good night.
Rage, rage against the dying of the light.

Philip Larkin (1922 – 85)
By his own account, Philip Larkin wrote prose
and verse 'ceaselessly' from the age of 18.
The ease with which it is possible to read his
poetry bears no relation to the effort he
employed. He was a persistent re-drafter and,
according to one biographer, the beginning of
a poem and its completion frequently lay far
apart. His often lugubrious tone is disliked by
many, but in a curious way that's what I find
attractive. There is a brutal realism to his feel

for late twentieth-century life. 'You do not come dramatically', he says in his poem to *Failure*. 'You have been here some time.' His *Letter to a friend about girls* was written in 1959, but long remained unpublished.

Ambulances

Closed like confessionals, they thread
Loud noons of cities, giving back
None of the glances they absorb.
Light glossy grey, arms on a plaque,
They come to rest at any kerb:
All streets in time are visited.

Then children strewn on steps or road,
Or women coming from the shops
Past smells of different dinners, see
A wild white face that overtops
Red stretcher-blankets momently
As it is carried in and stowed,

And sense the solving emptiness
That lies just under all we do,
And for a second get it whole,
So permanent and blank and true.
The fastened doors recede, *Poor soul*,
They whisper at their own distress;

For borne away in deadened air
May go the sudden shut of loss
Round something nearly at an end,
And what cohered in it across
The years, the unique random blend
Of families and fashions, there

At last begin to loosen. Far
From the exchange of love to lie
Unreachable inside a room
The traffic parts to let go by
Brings closer what is left to come,
And dulls to distance all we are.

Letter to a friend about girls
After comparing lives with you for years
I see how I've been losing: all the while
I've met a different gauge of girl from yours.
Grant that, and all the rest makes sense as well:
My mortification at your pushovers,
Your mystification at my fecklessness —
Everything proves we play in separate leagues.
Before, I couldn't credit your intrigues
Because I thought all girls the same, but yes,
You bag real birds, though they're from alien
　　covers.

Now I believe your staggering skirmishes
In train, tutorial and telephone booth,
The wife whose husband watched away matches
While she behaved so badly in a bath,
And all the rest who beckon from that world
Described on Sundays only, where to want
Is straightway to be wanted, seek to find,
And no one gets upset or seems to mind
At what you say to them, or what you don't:
A world where all the nonsense is annulled,
And beauty is accepted slang for yes.
But equally, haven't you noticed mine?
They have their world, not much compared with
　　yours,

261

But where they work, and age, and put off
  men
By being unattractive, or too shy,
Or having morals — anyhow, none give in:
Some of them go quite rigid with disgust
At anything but marriage: that's all lust
And so not worth considering; they begin
Fetching your hat, so that you have to lie

Till everything's confused: you mine away
For months, both of you, till the collapse
  comes
Into remorse, tears, and wondering why
You ever start such boring barren games
— But there, don't mind my *saeva indignation*:
I'm happier now I've got things clear, although
It's strange we never meet each other's sort:
There should be equal chances, I'd've thought.
Must finish now. One day perhaps I'll know
What makes you be so lucky in your ratio

— One of those 'more things', could it be?
Horatio.

Maya Angelou (1928 –)
The late James Baldwin said about Maya
Angelou: 'Black, bitter and beautiful, she
speaks of our survival.' Little more needs to
be said.

  She speaks for the brutalised, the oppressed,
the enslaved and the dispossessed and she
does it with great compassion. Her work
seems to suggest that against all the odds
people can survive and that they can triumph.

Maya Angelou's poems are born in the
great storytelling tradition of the black
American south. Her voice is authentic and
honest. She writes about hate and hardship
and violence, but her poet's eyes are filled
with hope and love and the glory of freedom.

The rhythm is all her own, although it owes
a great deal to the street talk and the church
singing and preaching of black America. What
also distinguishes Maya Angelou's work
though is her irrepressible humour. Even when
she writes about sadness or pain, her poems
are never less than a celebration of life in its
infinite variety.

Caged bird

A free bird leaps
on the back of the wind
and floats downstream
till the current ends
and dips his wing
in the orange sun rays
and dares to claim the sky.

But a bird that stalks
down his narrow cage
can seldom see through
his bars of rage
his wings are clipped and
his feet are tied
so he opens his throat to sing.

The caged bird sings
with a fearful trill

of things unknown
but longed for still
and his tune is heard
on the distant hill
for the caged bird
sings of freedom.

The free bird thinks of another breeze
and the trade winds soft through the sighing
    trees
and the fat worms waiting on a dawn-bright
    lawn
and he names the sky his own.

But a caged bird stands on the grave of
    dreams
his shadow shouts on a nightmare scream
his wings are clipped and his feet are tied
so he opens his throat to sing.

The caged bird sings
with a fearful trill
of things unknown
but longed for still
and his tune is heard
on the distant hill
for the caged bird
sings of freedom.

Still I rise
You may write me down in history
With your bitter, twisted lies,
You may trod me in the very dirt
But still, like dust, I'll rise.

Does my sassiness upset you?
Why are you beset with gloom?
'Cause I walk like I've got oil wells
Pumping in my living room.

Just like moons and like suns,
With the certainty of tides,
Just like hopes springing high,
Still I'll rise.

Did you want to see me broken?
Bowed head and lowered eyes?
Shoulders falling down like teardrops,
Weakened by my soulful cries.

Does my haughtiness offend you?
Don't you take it awful hard
'Cause I laugh like I've got gold mines
Diggin' in my own back yard.

You may shoot me with your words,
You may cut me with your eyes,
You may kill me with your hatefulness,
But still, like air, I'll rise.

Does my sexiness upset you?
Does it come as a surprise
That I dance like I've got diamonds
At the meeting of my thighs?

Out of the huts of history's shame
I rise
Up from a past that's rooted in pain
I rise

I'm a black ocean, leaping and wide,
Welling and swelling I bear in the tide.

Leaving behind nights of terror and fear
I rise
Into a daybreak that's wondrously clear
I rise
Bringing the gifts that my ancestors gave,
I am the dream and the hope of the slave.

I rise
I rise
I rise.

Derek Walcott (1930 –)

The popularity and stature of West Indian
poetry came long after I began learning poems
by rote as a child. Today its brilliance is
universally acknowledged. This poem is not
untypical of Derek Walcott's work. Like his
Caribbean contemporaries, he employs the
experience of conflict of heritage to take
protest almost to the point of epiphany.

Derek Walcott's plays and poetry achieved
an international reputation long before he won
the Nobel Prize for Literature two years ago.
But there's no question that the prize greatly
enhanced his stature as a poet and made
many more people aware of West Indian
poetry. Walcott, it goes without saying, is one
of its greatest exponents. A persistent theme
in the poetry from the islands is their
chequered colonial history and the attempt to
make sense of the present by understanding

the past. There is also the conflict of heritage, which Walcott himself expresses with such brutal honesty in one poem: 'Where shall I turn, divided to the vein.' *Tales of the Islands* should be read in its entirety.

From **Tales of the Islands**

CHAPTER IX 'LE LOUPGAROU'

A curious tale that threaded through the town
Through greying women sewing under eaves,
Was how his greed had brought old Le Brun
    down,
Greeted by slowly shutting jalousies
When he approached them in white linen suit,
Pink glasses, cork hat, and tap-tapping cane,
A dying man licensed to sell sick fruit,
Ruined by fiends with whom he'd made a
    bargain.
It seems one night, these Christian witches
    said,
He changed himself to an Alsatian hound,
A slavering lycanthrope hot on a scent,
But his own watchman dealt the thing a wound.
It howled and lugged its entrails, trailing wet
With blood, back to its doorstep, almost dead.

CHAPTER X 'ADIEU FOULARD . . . '

I watched the island narrowing the fine
Writing of foam around the precipices, then
The roads as small and casual as twine
Thrown on its mountains; I watched till the
    plane
Turned to the final north and turned above
The open channel with the grey sea between

267

The fishermen's islets until all that I love
Folded in cloud; I watched the shallow green
That broke in places where there would be
  reef,
The silver glinting on the fuselage, each mile
Dividing us and all fidelity strained
Till space would snap it. Then, after a while
I thought of nothing, nothing, I prayed, would
  change;
When we set down at Seawall it had rained.

A far cry from Africa
A wind is ruffling the tawny pelt
Of Africa, Kikuyu, quick as flies,
Batten upon the bloodstreams of the veldt.
Corpses are scattered through a paradise.
Only the worm, colonel of carrion, cries:
'Waste no compassion on these separate dead!'
Statistics justify and scholars seize
The salients of colonial policy.
What is that to the white child hacked in bed?
To savages, expendable as Jews?

Threshed out by beaters, the long rushes break
In a white dust of ibises whose cries
Have wheeled since civilization's dawn
From the parched river or beast-teeming plain.
The violence of beast on beast is read
As natural law, but upright man
Seeks his divinity with inflicting pain.
Delirious as these worried beasts, his wars
Dance to the tightened carcass of a drum,
While he calls courage still that native dread
Of the white peace contracted by the dead.

Again brutish necessity wipes its hands
Upon the napkin of a dirty cause, again
A waste of our compassion, as with Spain,
The gorilla wrestles with the superman.
I who am poisoned with the blood of both,
Where shall I turn, divided to the vein?
I who have cursed
The drunken officer of British rule, how choose
Between this Africa and the English tongue
    I love?
Betray them both, or give back what they give?
How can I face such slaughter and be cool?
How can I turn from Africa and live?

Ted Hughes (1930 –)

Our current Poet Laureate, Ted Hughes was
born in West Yorkshire, where he led an
outdoor life and developed his keen interest in
the beautiful, but violent, natural world.

His poetry is renowned for the violence of
its imagery and has been criticised by some
for its 'brutality'. None can deny, however,
the power of his poetry, as demonstrated in *A
sparrow hawk*.

A sparrow hawk

Slips from your eye-corner — overtaking
Your first thought.

Through your mulling gaze over haphazard
    earth
The sun's cooled carbon wing
Whets the eyebeam.

Those eyes in their helmet
Still wired direct
To the nuclear core — they alone

Laser the lark-shaped hole
In the lark's song.

You find the fallen spurs, among soft ashes.

And maybe you find him

Materialized by twilight and dew
Still as a listener —

The warrior

Blue shoulder-cloak wrapped about him
Leaning, hunched,
Among the oaks of the harp.

Sylvia Plath (1932 – 63)

An American from Boston, Plath met her
future husband, Ted Hughes, at Cambridge.
After a time together in America, they
returned to England in 1959. Her first
collection of poetry, *The Colossus*, was
published in 1960. In 1963, just a few weeks
after the publication of her novel, *The Bell
Far*, she took her own life in London.

You're

Clownlike, happiest on your hands,
Feet to the stars, and moon-skulled,
Gilled like a fish. A common-sense

Thumbs-down on the dodo's mode.
Wrapped up in yourself like a spool,
Trawling your dark as the owls do.
Mute as a turnip from the Fourth
Of July to All Fools' Day,
O high-riser, my little loaf.

Vague as fog and looked for like mail.
Farther off than Australia.
Bent-backed Atlas, our travelled prawn.
Snug as a bud and at home
Like a sprat in a pickle jug.
A creel of eels, all ripples.
Jumpy as a Mexican bean.
Right, like a well-done sum.
A celan slate, with your own face on.

Crossing the water
Black lake, black boat, two black, cut-paper people.
Where do the black trees go that drink here?
Their shadows must cover Canada.

A little light is filtering from the water flowers.
Their leaves do not wish us to hurry:
They are round and flat and full of dark advice.

Cold worlds shake from the oar.
The spirit of blackness is in us, it is in the fishes.
A snag is lifting a valedictory, pale hand;

271

Stars open among the lilies.
Are you not blinded by such expressionless sirens?
This is the silence of astounded souls.

Seamus Heaney (1939 –)

It was obvious from my very first visit there
that few countries are as proud of their writers
and their literature as Ireland. And while the
news quite properly concentrates on the
politics of Ireland, Irish writing has always had
a profound influence on the life of the
country and beyond.

Today the literature is as brilliant and
powerful as it ever was, fired in the crucible
of violence and unrest and lightened only by
tantalising glimpses of peace and normality.
Irish writers describe the condition of their
compatriots and their country with realism
and honesty, and invariably with humour.
Seamus Heaney, who won the Nobel Prize for
Literature in 1993, illustrates all this
eloquently.

Three drawings

I THE POINT

'Those were the days —
booting a leather football
truer and farther
than you ever expected!

It went rattling
hard and fast
over daisies and benweeds,
it thumped

but it sang too,
a kind of dry, ringing
foreclosure of sound.
Or else, a great catch

and a cry from the touch-line
to *Point-her!* That spring
and unhampered smash-through!
Was it you

or the ball that kept going
beyond you, amazingly
higher and higher
and ruefully free?'

II THE PULSE
The effortlessness
of a spinning reel. One quick
flick of the wrist
and your minnow sped away

whispering and silky
and nimbly laden.
It seemed to be all rise
and shine, the very opposite

of uphill going — it was pure
duration, and when it ended,
the pulse of the cast line
entering water

was smaller in your hand
than the remembered heartbeat

of a bird. Then, after all of that
runaway give, you were glad

when you reeled in and found
yourself strung, heel-tip
to rod-tip, into the river's
steady purchase and thrum.

III A HAUL

The one that got away
from Thor and the giant Hymer
was the world-serpent itself.
The god had baited his line

with an ox-head, spun it high
and plunged it into the depths.
But the big haul came to an end
when Thor's foot went through the boards

and Hymer panicked and cut
the line with a bait-knife. Then
roll-over, turmoil, whiplash!
A Milky Way in the water.

The hole he smashed in the boat
opened, the way Thor's head
opened out there on the sea.
He felt at one with space,

unroofed and obvious —
surprised in his empty arms
like some fabulous high-catcher
coming down with the ball.

Notes

The publishers gratefully acknowledge permission to reproduce the following copyright material.

'The house of hospitalities', 'In Tenebris I', 'Great things' and 'In time of 'The breaking of nations' ' from *The Complete Poems* by Thomas Hardy. Reprinted by permission of Macmillan.

'Bredon Hill', 'Last Poems, XXXIV, The first of May', 'Untitled verse' and 'Easter hymn' by A. E. Housman. Reprinted by permission of The Society of Authors.

'To Ireland in the coming times', 'Easter 1916' and 'When you are old' from *The Collected Poems of W. B. Yeats*. Reprinted by permission of A. P. Watt Ltd on behalf of Michael Yeats.

'Tarantella' and 'The garden party' by Hilaire Belloc. Reprinted by permission of The Peters Fraser and Dunlop Group Limited on behalf of The Estate of Hilaire Belloc ©: as printed in the original volume, *Complete Verse* by Hilaire Belloc.

'John Mouldy' and 'All that's past' by Walter De la Mare. Reprinted by permission of The Society of Authors.

Index of first lines

284

Other titles in the Charnwood Library Series:

LEGACIES
Janet Dailey

The sequel to THE PROUD AND THE FREE. It is twenty years since the feud within his family began, but Lije Stuart, son of the Cherokee chief The Blade, had never forgotten the killing of his grandfather. Now, a promising legal career beckons, and also the love of his childhood sweetheart, Diane Parmalee, the daughter of a US Army officer. Yet as it reawakens, their love is beset by the beginning of civil war.

'L' IS FOR LAWLESS
Sue Grafton

World War II fighter pilot Johnny Lee had died and his grandson was trying to claim military funeral benefits, but none of the authorities have any record of Fighter J. Lee. Was the old man once a US spy? When PI Kinsey Millhone is asked to straighten things out, she finds herself pursued by a psychopath bearing a forty-year-old grudge . . .

BLOOD LINES
Ruth Rendell

This is a collection of long and short stories by Ruth Rendell that will linger in the mind.

THE SUN IN GLORY
Harriet Hudson

When industrialist William Potts sets himself to build a flying machine, his adopted daughter, Rosie, works through the years as his mechanic. In 1906 Pegasus is almost ready, and onto the scene comes Jake Smith, a man who has as deep a love of the air as Rosie herself. But Jake sparks off a deadly rivalry, and the triumph of flight twists into tragedy.

A WOMAN SCORNED
M. R. O'Donnell

Five years after the tragedy that ruined her fifteenth birthday, Judith Carty returns to Castle Moore and resumes her flirtation with its heir, Rick Bellingham. The tragic events of the past forge a special bond between the young couple, but there are those who have a vested interest in the failure of the romance.

PLAINER STILL
Catherine Cookson

Following the success of her previous collection of essays and poems, LET ME MAKE MYSELF PLAIN, Catherine Cookson has compiled a further selection of thoughts, recollections, and observations on life — and death — together with another collection of the poems she prefers to describe as 'prose on short lines'.

THE LOST WORLD
Michael Crichton
The successor to JURASSIC PARK.
It is now six years since the secret disaster
of Jurassic Park, when that extraordinary
dream of science and imagination came to
a crashing end — the dinosaurs destroyed,
and the park dismantled. There are rumours
that something has survived . . .

MORNING, NOON & NIGHT
Sidney Sheldon
When Harry Stanford, one of the wealthiest
men in the world, mysteriously drowns, it
sets off a chain of events that reverberates
around the globe. At the family gathering
following the funeral, a beautiful young
woman appears, claiming to be Harry's
daughter. Is she genuine, or is she an
impostor?

FACING THE MUSIC
Jayne Torvill and Christopher Dean
The world's most successful and popular
skating couple tell their own story, from their
working-class childhoods in Nottingham to
world stardom. Finally, they describe how
they created their own show, FACE THE
MUSIC, with a superb corps of international
ice dancers.

ORANGES AND LEMONS
Jeanne Whitmee

When Shirley Rayner is evacuated from London's East End, she finds herself billeted with the theatre's most romantic couple, Tony and Leonie Darrent. She becomes firm friends with their daughter, Imogen, and the two girls dream of making their names on the stage. But they have forgotten the very different backgrounds from which they come.

HALF HIDDEN
Emma Blair

Holly Morgan, a nurse in a hospital on Nazi-occupied Jersey, falls in love with a young German doctor, Peter Schmidt, and is racked by guilt. Can their love survive the future together or will the war destroy all their hopes and dreams?

THE GREAT TRAIN ROBBERY
Michael Crichton

In Victorian London, where lavish wealth and appalling poverty exist side by side, one man navigates both worlds with ease. Rich, handsome and ingenious, Edward Pierce preys on the most prominent of the well-to-do as he cunningly orchestrates the crime of his century.